# THE GREAT AWAKENING

**Volume - VII**

A series of superbly informative and prophetic messages,
downloaded and transcribed originally as newsletters by

## Sister Thedra

These precious messages are reprinted herein.

ISBN: 978-1-7363418-9-6

# Contents

# Mission Statement

Give the truth to the world. Let it be received where it will. Many will read the messages. Some will accept the truth, others will read through curiosity, a few will ridicule. Yet to all is the truth given, and to all remains the power of choice.

The hope of the world in these times is in spiritualizing all forms of activity---promoting understanding through love and service. These must be the watchwords if the world is to come into lasting peace. We are trying to influence a world that is going astray and could cause undreamed of suffering. We are trying to overcome the thought of materialists and to bring a spiritual outlook into the earthly life. We need the help of all on earth who can think in spiritual terms. The great battle to be fought now is between the spiritual and the material, between idealism and carnalism. You can help by spreading the word---we are asking that you help because the battle may be long and the victory far away.

Halls of Light is not allied with any sect, denomination, political entity, organization, neither endorses nor opposes any cause. There are no dues for membership. Halls of Light is self-supporting through its own voluntary contributions. Halls of Light has but one purpose: to help through encouragement and understanding...

To contact the publishers or to obtain copies of our other books, please contact us at email: goldtown11@gmail.com

**Esu Jesus Sananda**

This reproduction is from an actual photograph taken on June 1st, 1961, in Chichen Itza, Yucatan, by one of thirty archaeologists working in the area at the time. Sananda appeared in visible, tangible body and permitted His photograph to be taken.

# THE SIBORS PORTIONS

## Part #26

### Sister Saboni

Blest of My being: I am thy sister Saboni - and I come unto thee that ye may go into my home land prepared for the work which ye shall do within that country - and within the place wherein they have their sayings - and say them with regularity -- Now it is given unto me to be the guardian of that country - and they shall come to know me - and they shall be awakened! And they shall give of themself unto me and unto the Father which has sent me -- And they shall be as ones which shall come to know the Father even as I know Him -- And they shall bow down to no man - for it is fortuned unto me and my fellow beings from the Inner Temple to be of the "Order of Light" wherein we see and know that which has been fortuned Her of the Father - and that which she (Italy) has fortuned unto Herself - - So be it that She shall be quickened unto the Light we shed upon Her ---

And now ye shall be my hands made manifest unto the people of Italy and Spain -- For it is given unto me to say that which is given unto me of the Father which they have forgotten -- So be it that they shall receive that which I have prepared for them - and so be it as follows:

Blest of my being: I am thy sister of Light from the place wherein the Father is -- I have come out of the silence that ye may remember thy being with the Father and Mother before ye went out

1

into the world of darkness -- At that time ye made a covenant with them - "That ye should not forget - and that ye should return unto them!" Now ye have found thyself a part of the world of darkness - wherein ye remember them only in thy "longing for perfection" and love ---

And they which have held thee within their hearts of the golden flame have watched and guided thee and sustained thee thru thy sorrow and suffering -- Now ye shall be made to remember them with whom ye have been in the Inner Temple before taking upon thyself garments of the Earth - and which have hung heavily upon thee -- Thy bodies of flesh shall be quickened and they shall no longer weigh thee down -- And ye shall stand forth in bodies of light even as we - for we are free from the gravitation of the Earth - and the attraction of the Moon -- So too shall ye be ---

And now it is given unto one to be sent unto thee from the place wherein I am - and they shall give unto thee as it is given unto them of the Father - for ye shall know that which has been kept for thee - and ye shall be as the Father - for He has given unto thee a bountiful inheritance - and ye have groveled within the mire for a poor pittance -- Ye shall bow only to the Father and unto them which He shall send unto thee to deliver thee out of thy bondage of darkness - --

Ye have said thy prayers as sayings - and as nothing more! Ye comprehend not their meaning -- And that profits thee naught! for the Father hears not that which is said as if it were operated within a coin machine -- Ye have the fortune to know that which ye say and to comprehend the meaning thereof -- Ye shall be given a mind to comprehend that which shall be given unto thee of the Father - Son and Holy Ghost ---

Ye shall partake of the new dispensation in wisdom and mercy - for it is given unto man of this "age of light" to walk and talk freely with the ones from the realms of light -- And they shall be as ones which can say: "I know my Father and Mother from whence I came - and I know whither I goest" - and therein is the greatest of wisdom!

So be ye prepared for the new dawn which is come - and ye shall partake of the "Manna from Heaven" - and I shall give unto thee of my love and wisdom - of my strength and mercy ---

So be it that I shall watch over thee - and be ye quickened unto my presence - for I am nigh unto thee - and the Father – Son and Holy Ghost has given me passport unto thee -- And so be it and Beleis -- I am thy sister and Servant in the Light of the Christ -- Sister Saboni - of The Emerald Cross ---

## Beautealu

Blest of my being: Ye shall now receive of the one and only Beautealu - and that which he has prepared for them in the name of the Father - Son and Holy Ghost -- So be it and Beleis -- Be ye at poise for I am with thee that ye may receive of thy own account - and so be it that I shall sit and counsel thee - and ye shall be as my hand unto them which as yet do not know me -- So be it and Beleis -- Sananda ---

Blest of my being: I am he which is known in the place wherein all things are known as the "Son of the Posied" ---

3

And I give unto my Father credit - for He has given unto the Earth of Himself that She might be brot into Her fullness - and fulfill Her mission within the place wherein She shall go -- For it is given unto Her to have a new berth which has been prepared for Her -- And in the time which is near She shall move out as a ship slips out of its port into the high seas - and She shall be brot safely into Her new berth ---

And many which are of the school of the Losoloes are preparing Her for Her new part and the people of the Earth shall too have a new part -- And it is our part which has been given unto us of the Father to prepare the people of the Earth for their new place and their new part ---

So be it that we shall do all within our power which is within the law to bring them into their full inheritance which is given unto them of the Father ---

And now ye shall be told that there are some among thee that is being prepared to stand upon the high Holy Mount and see that which shall occur - and as it occurs -- And so be it that ye shall come to know the work of the Father and them which are sent to prepare thee that ye may be like unto Him ---

For it is given unto many which has come out from the place wherein He is to be among thee to prepare thee that ye may not know chaos and suffering -- For they which are not mindful of the Father and them which are sent at this time to sibor thee are sure to be as ones which have thrown their life belts overboard - and they shall cry Lord! Lord! and they shall be late! And they shall remember that which they heeded not! So be ye wise and call unto the Father while

4

we are within hearing and at thy service - for the day shall come when we shall again be deaf unto thy call ---

For the <u>Alert</u>! has gone out thru the Cosmos and ye shall be foolish indeed to turn a deaf ear -- I am at thy service in the Name of the Father - Son and Holy Ghost - Amen and Selah --

Beautealu - Son of the Posied - and of the School of 7 Rays --

**The Posied**

Blest of my being: I am the Posied - father of Beautealu - with whom I am come into the Earth that She shall be prepared ---

If ye could but open thy eyes and see as we see and know as we know - ye should be up and about the Father's business - for so vast is the business of the Father that we stand in awe - and we too stand in awe and humility at His command and Love and Mercy ---

For it is given unto us of the Inner Temple to obey and <u>respect</u> the command - and the law which is given unto us -- And we make haste to carry out any command given unto us of the Most Worthy Grand Master which is the one to whom we are responsible in the · great mission which has brot us to the Earth -- And we shall not leave Her until it is completed -- For it is given unto us to complete that which is entrusted unto us to do -- And so be it that we shall prepare some from among thee who are ready to be groomed for the Inner Temple ---

And there are some which have waited for many sons for this day that they may enter into the Inner Temple - and so shall their

5

waiting come to an end - with love and wisdom -- So be it and Selah---

I am at thy service in the Name of the Most High -- I am the Posied - of the Emerald Cross --

Recorded by Sister Thedra ---

# Part #27

Blest of my being: Ye shall receive of that which has been prepared for them by the one and only Posied -- And he shall give unto them that which is prepared for thee - and it shall be given unto thee of the Father - Son and Holy Ghost -- And so be it and Beleis ---

## The Posied

Blest of my presence: Ye shall give my words unto "them" which await them -- And so be it that they shall profit thereby -- for it is given unto me of the Father - that I may give unto them - that they may be alert unto our presence - and unto the plan which is given unto us to fulfill -- For it is now come that ye shall awaken into the "New Age of Light" -- And ye shall prepare thyself that ye may BE BROT OUT OF DARKNESS INTO THE LIGHT ---

And we cry from every corner of the Earth: <u>PREPARE!</u> <u>PREPARE</u>! for it is for that reason that we have left our place of abode and come into the Earth wherein is darkness!

And be ye mindful of us - and that which we are offering thee at this time -- What more can we do than offer thee salvation from thy own bondage of darkness - suffering and sorrow?

Now shall ye be so foolish as to reject it? If so ye shall suffer the consequence according to the law -- And we comprehend the law - and as we see with greater vision we thy brothers which have gone the Royal Road and we know the pitfalls and we know wherein the danger lieth -- We are <u>alert</u> and we endeavor to alert thee that ye may not suffer more - and that there may be order - and less chaos

For there shall be great changes within thy Earth and ye shall be removed -- And will ye not be prepared when the hour strikes?

For as ye accept my words have ye accepted me - and as ye accept me ye have accepted the Father which has sent me unto thee -- And there are many sent from the place wherein I abide - that they may prepare thee -- Wherein is it said: "As ye accept the Messengers of the Father - ye accept Him?" So be ye alert unto the call which has gone out thru the Cosmos -- For there shall be no hiding place -- And as ye are prepared so shall ye receive and be it such as ye have prepared thyself to receive ---

And shall it not profit thee to increase thy capacity for receiving? So be it and Selah –

I am thy Older Brother which proffers thee a hand in the Name of the Most High -- And so be it and Selah -- The Posied - of the Emerald Cross ---

Blest of my being: Ye shall now receive of the one and only Beautealu - son of the Posied - and he shall give unto thee that which ye shall give unto them which are to receive of his words which are given unto him of the Father - Son and Holy Ghost -- For he has prepared a part which is designed to awaken them which are yet asleep -- And for that has he given of himself and his love and wisdom - so shall it profit them -- And may they receive that which is proffered them in Love - Mercy and Wisdom -- So be it and Beleis --

## Beautealu

Blest of my Being and of my Presence - for I am come unto thee that ye may give unto them this message - and so be it that it is given unto me to give unto them which are prepared to receive it -- So be it that ye shall be blest of the Father - that ye have been my hands made manifest unto them -- And so be it that they shall awaken unto the "New Age of Light" and they shall know us their Sibors - and they shall be as ones awakened from the dead - so be it and Selah -- I am come unto the Earth from the place wherein the Father is - that His will may be done within the Earth - and that ye shall awaken from thy slumber which ye have poured out for thyself to the eons of thy Earthly journey ---

And ye have been bound within darkness by the black dragon which shall be removed forever -- He shall no longer hold forth within the Earth! I say unto thee that we offer thee thy freedom - ye have but to accept it - and as ye will it so be it - and ye have but to seek the light within thy eternal breast - the Light which never fails -- For it is now the Age of Light - when ye shall stand forth within the Light of the Christ - and ye shall know thyself as ye are known -- And for this have ye waited -- And as ye call out for Light and Wisdom ye shall be heard and answered and given accordingly - as ye are capable of receiving - and as ye are prepared ---

And so be it that it shall profit thee to call unto the Father and as ye call many shall be sent that ye may be sustained in thy search for the open gate -- And it shall swing wide before thee -- And so be ye prepared to receive us thy Brothers from the Inner Temple - and wherein we are prepared to receive thee -- And so be it and Selah --

I am thy Older Brother Beautealu - Son of the Posied - of the School of the 7 Rays ---

Blest of my being: Ye shall now receive of our beloved Sister of Light - Sister Saboni - guardian of Italy -- And ye shall give unto them that which she has prepared for thee - and ye shall give unto them that which she has received of our Father which has given her passport unto thee ---

## Sister Saboni

Blest of my presence - and of the Father - which has given unto me permission to come unto thee from out of the silence and from the place wherein the Father is -- I am come that I might add my love and light unto that of my Brothers and Sisters of Light - that all may come to know their inheritance and to receive it - which has been kept for them -- And we which have been fortuned that which was given unto us as our heritage are now in a position to offer thee a hand in Love - Mercy and Wisdom ---

I am the Mother of Italy - I have guarded Her - and I have given of my love and knowledge unto Her -- And yet She has not awakened unto Her heritage! For it is given unto Her to be of the old order - and She is bound by the old law - and by that which She shall be fortuned to break -- For She shall have the yoke lifted - and She shall be as ones loosed from the bands which has bound them to the post of prison -- And they shall be glad that they have received of the new dispensation - and of the portion which we of the higher realms are preparing to give unto Her ---

And we are grooming many to receive of the new seed - so be it that the harvest shall be a bountiful one -- And it shall be cause for great rejoicing thruout the Father's Kingdom -- And so be it and Selah ---

And it is so planned that "One" shall be sent unto them which shall be unto them my hands and my feet and my mouth -- For out of their mouth shall come that which I shall give unto them to say - and they shall be unto them that which the Father would have them be -- And they shall raise the dead - and heal the sick - and make the blind to see -- And therein is the plan which has been given unto me to give unto the One which shall be sent unto them -- And wherein they shall be prepared for that part which shall be fortuned unto them ---

And as I have given unto this one to receive of that which I shall give unto them thru the Love - Mercy and Wisdom of our Father - so shall I give unto them wisdom to accept the One which shall go out in the Name of the Father - Son and Holy Ghost and in the service of the Christ -- And so be it that they shall receive of His Love and Mercy of the Earth - and thru them shall the Earth receive of their Light that She may come into Her own inheritance - so be it and Selah -- I am thy Sister Saboni - of the Emerald Cross –

Recorded by Sister Thedra of the Emerald Cross ---

# Part #28

Blest of my being: Ye shall now receive that which is prepared for them by one which is known as The Phonecian - and it is given unto him to be in the place wherein I am - and wherein are many which await thy coming -- He will give unto thee thy part separate and apart -- For he has much for them which are of a mind to receive it -- And so be it given unto them in the Name of the Father - Son and Holy Ghost - and Beleis ---

## The Phonecian

Beloved one - which shall be my hand unto them: I am come that these words may reach them who are prepared to receive them - We which are within this place are from the Temple of Osiris - and we have been entrusted with the plan which is to be brot into fruit-- And now we are grooming many which shall have part in its fulfillment -- And they shall be brot into the place wherein they shall partake of the revelation which has been given unto us which have long awaited this day -- And it shall be given unto me to wait for them which shall be brot into this place which has served as a place of science and philosophy for many centuries ---

And from this place has many initiates gone out into the world to bring into fruit that which has been given within this place -- And now we who reside within this place have sent out a proclamation that all who so desire and have prepared themself for this work shall be brot immediately! For it is come that all which have part within this plan shall be prepared now! ---

And they shall be groomed for their part and returned into the world that they may know that which is fortuned unto her in this Age of Light ---

There are great things in store for them which are ready for such training - and for this time have we come when men must either move on into greater realms - or they shall be put into the compound wherein they may sleep until they awaken of their own accord -- For the hour has struck that the Earth shall move into more light - and She shall not give unto the sleepers comfort and footing - for She shall progress on Her appointed course and they shall not be unto Her a poison ---

Now ye shall come to know me for I shall say unto thee that which shall serve to arouse thee from thy lethargy -- And to alert thee - for many are reaching out a hand that ye may find thy way into the place wherein ye may be prepared for the Inner Temple wherein "All things are known"---

And it shall be my part to prepare thee for that -- And ye shall be glad for thy preparation for it is given unto us to see that which is before thee -- And it shall behoove thee to prepare thyself -- And so be it and Beleis and Selah ---

I am thy Brother of the Secret City wherein ye may gain thy passport into the Inner Temple -- So be it and Selah -- The Phonecian of the Emerald Cross -- (Here I am requested to say the Phonecian is not Paul the Venetian - - Thedra)

Blest of my being: Be ye prepared to receive that which is prepared by our brother which has revealed himself as the one called

13

the "Aryan" - for he has prepared a part which shall be given unto them -- And ye shall be unto him his hands that they may receive it -- And be ye blest of him and that which he has kept for thee -- So be it and Beleis ---

## The Aryan

Blessed one whom I shall ask to be my hands unto them - I shall give unto thee that which I have kept for thee ---

And now I shall give thee that which is meant for them which are prepared to receive it -- And may they see that which it contains within it - for it is given unto many to look and not see -- If they but search they shall be greatly rewarded ---

Now I say unto them - that I have come out of the place wherein I have been for one purpose only - and that is to fulfill the plan which has been revealed unto me in its entirety and which is unfolding before thee ---

And be ye diligent in thy search - for there are many signs and many places wherein ye may see the "writing on the wall"-- I am fortuned to be the "Wanderer! -- I have wandered across the face of the Earth since our beloved Master Sananda - Jesus of Nazareth - was upon Golgotha -- And He said to me: "Thou shall tarry until I return"-- And so have I - and so has He returned that the new day may bear fruit -- And that He may fulfill His mission and keep His covenant with the Father ---

And now ye shall come to know him as I know him - for long has it been since first we met -- And when he gave me the command to tarry within the Earth I knew not how long! Now it is come that I see the wisdom on my waiting -- And I am glad the day of the new dispensation is come - when we each and every one shall move into a field afar and wherein we may receive that which has been given unto us as our inheritance -- For now it is given unto us to have many brothers of Light sent from the higher realms of Light that we may be brot into the place which is prepared for us ---

It has been given unto me to be the "Wayfarer" and I have given unto thee of my love and of my wisdom within reason and within the law -- Yet I have been bound by the law of the old order -- Now I am free in the new dispensation - and I can speak freely - for I am within the place wherein our Lord and Master Sananda is - and He has given unto me of His mercy and His grace that I may have more freedom - that I may give unto thee ---

Now it is come that I shall speak thru our blessed sister which has given of herself that the Father's Will may be done thru her - and by her -- And ye shall receive it in the time which is near for it shall be given unto one of our blessed brothers which has held out a hand that ye may receive that which is given unto thee -- For they are messengers of the Father and they shall be richly blest - and they shall be lifted up - and they shall sit on the right hand of God the Father - for He remembers them which do His Will and which are His hands made manifest --

And will ye not accept that which they have given unto thee of the ones which have so generously reached out to thee that ye may know that which is come about thru their love and grace and mercy?

For the gate unto the Inner Temple is now open unto thee - and they are the pointers along the way - and ye have but to follow within their footsteps for every step of the way they know - and they are the brothers which have opened the way that ye may find thy way - - And will ye not give ear unto them and be up and about thy way - for it is given unto me to know the longing and the sorrow which ye shall experience if ye do not follow the one which has said: "I shall come again to claim my own" –

Now that he is come - and He is crying from all the mountain tops of the Earth - will it not profit thee to listen? Ye shall come as little children - for all thy opinions and all thy airs shall avail thee nothing - they shall be as tacks in thy shoes!

So be ye as a child and ask the Father for comprehension - and a greater capacity for learning ---

For ye have not sought these things which should profit thee -- "In all thy getting ye have not gotten wisdom!"

So be it that it too shall be added unto the rest of thy gifts which shall be given of the Father which has kept thy inheritance for thee -- And so be it that ye shall become of age - and that ye shall receive thy inheritance in full -- So be it and Belcis ---

I am the Aryan - known as the Wanderer - of the School of The Seven Rays --- Recorded by Sister Thedra - of The School of The Seven Rays --

# Part #29

Blest of my being: Be ye prepared to receive that which has been prepared for thee by the one and only Posied - for he has given of himself that ye may receive that which he has prepared for thee -- And it shall be given unto them which shall receive it in the Name of the Father - Son and Holy Ghost -- And so be it and Beleis –

## The Posied

Blest of my presence and of my being: For I am come unto thee that ye may receive that which is given unto me of the Father - and that ye may give unto them which are prepared to receive of the Father - - And ye shall be my hands made manifest unto them - And so be it that they shall come to know me - and the part which they shall have with me -- For it is my part to prepare them for that which is before them -- They have no comprehension of that which they shall encounter! And for that reason are many sent that they may be

## prepared ---

And now ye shall say unto them that which I shall give unto thee and it is given in the Name of the Father - Son and Holy Ghost-- So be ye prepared even as I am prepared to receive of the Father---

Blest are thy hands for they shall know no sorrow - for it is given unto me to give unto thee as I have received of the Father - and I shall remember thee as He has remembered me -- And so be it and Selah ---

Be ye which are to receive my words - blest of my presence and of the Father - Son and Holy Ghost -- I am the one which has been sent that ye may be prepared to receive of thy new part which shall be given unto thee -- And ye which have prepared thyself shall partake of the glory and the riches of the new Earth - and of Her blessing which She shall be prepared to give unto thee -- For She shall be given a new place within the firmaments and She shall be cleansed and purified and every atom shall be renewed -- And She shall receive the new seed which is now being prepared -- and She shall be as a garden and She shall give unto the new seed a place of abode ---

And ye shall be prepared in love and wisdom to partake of the bounties and of Her inheritance -- For it is given unto me to know that which She shall become - and that which ye may become if ye but will it so -- And none can command thee -- Yet ye may prepare thyself that ye may know such joy as She the New Earth can give unto thee -- The garden of the new Earth shall arise from the floor of the Atlantic (ocean) and it shall raise its lofty peaks some eighteen thousand feet (ref: Prophecies from other worlds of 1954) and it shall be given unto man to be blest by the strength they shall find within these mountains - for there shall be wonders untold in them -- And ye shall be prepared to partake of Her strength and Her beauty if ye will it so ---

And it is my part to prepare the Lotus for its habitation - and to prepare the habitation for the Lotus ---

So be it that there shall be many changes within the Earth within the time which is near -- And it shall be the better part of wisdom to be alert and prepared - for it shall come upon thee within the twinkling of an eye - and ye shall be prepared or found wanting -- And it is sad indeed to be found wanting - for I have heard the cry of them which are not prepared and it is indeed sad -- And for that do we cry unto thee to prepare thyself -- And forget not that we shall not be content to let thee forget -- For we have come out from the Father that ye may be prepared - and may it be the way of the wise! And the way of the Father Who has willed it -- And so be it and Selah ---

I am thy Brother in the service of the Christ which ye shall come to know -- So be it and Selah ---

The Posied of the Emerald Cross --

Blest of my being: Be prepared to receive of the one and only Beautealu - for he has prepared a part for them -- And ye shall be his hands made manifest unto them -- So be it that it shall profit them - and it shall be given unto them of the Father – Son and Holy Ghost -- Amen and Beleis ---

**Beautealu**

Blest of my being: Be ye blest of my presence – and of the Father which has sent me unto thee that my words may be given unto them which await them – And blest shall they be which receive them for I am come that they may be blest – and that whey may come to know the Father as we thy Sibors know Him – And so be it that ye shall give unto them these words – and ye shall be blest of the Father – Son and Holy Ghost – And so be it and Selah ---

Blessed ones which are prepared to receive these words which are given unto me of the Father - Son and Holy Ghost - and who are prepared for the new dispensation: I say unto thee that there are many from the higher realms within thy midst which are watching thy progress and which stand ready to give unto thee that which shall profit thee to receive -- And ye have but to ask and give them credence - for now it has been said over and over that it is time to alert thyself - and so it is!

And yet ye are sluggish - ye have not comprehended the greatness of our message unto thee - for ye have been unto thyself traitor - ye have not alerted thyself -- Will it be so in the day of thy discomfort and of thy sorrow when ye shall say Lord! Lord! Deliver me! And have ye not been offered thy deliverance? And shall ye wait until disaster is upon thee? For it shall come - sure as the dawn! And so be it that ye have been given warning -- Ye have been offered thy freedom -- And ye have but to accept it in the Name of the Father - Son and Holy Ghost -- So be it and Selah ---

Blest shall they be which shall accept the offer which shall be thy inheritance of the Father -- And for that has the new dispensation been given unto thee -- Ye have given no thot unto thy "Fortune of Light" and that which ye shall become by the Love and Grace of the Father and the Brothers and Sisters of Light which are sent of the Father that ye may receive: of His mercy ---

Be ye as wise as a serpent and give ear unto that which we say unto thee - for the cry is sounded from every corner of the Earth! Yet thy feet are leaden and ye have thy fingers in thy ears -- And ye have not stirred thyself -- So be ye in the place wherein ye are prepared to receive that which shall be given unto thee - for that which shall be given unto thee shall serve to awaken thee and it shall stand thee four square -- And so be it and Beleis --

Are ye not in the "School of Earth" to learn? And will ye not move into another school of an advanced order? For it is now come that the Earth shall <u>not</u> give footing unto the "sleepers" and "laggards" -- And as ye will it so be it unto thee -- For we thy Sibors of the New Order have said that which has been given unto us of the Father and that which should be sufficient unto thee - and sad indeed it is that ye have not heard - for we are as ones crying in the wilderness -- Yet ye shall awaken! And ye shall pick thyself up by thy toes - and ye shall go into the place which ye have prepared for thyself - be it great or small - as ye are prepared

And now it is given unto me to come unto thee and I shall sibor thee in truth and wisdom in the Name of the Most High ---

I am thy servant and Older Brother - Son of the Posied - and of the School of the Seven Rays -- Beautealu ---

Recorded by Sister Thedra - School of The Seven Rays --

# Part #30

Blest of my being; Ye shall now receive that which the one and only Marshea has prepared for them - and ye shall be unto him his hands made manifest -. And so shall it be given unto thee of the Father - Son and Holy Ghost -- Amen and Beleis ---

## Marshea

Blest of my being and of my presence: Ye shall be given that which the Father has given unto me that ye may give unto them which are to receive my words - and of that which I have for them -- And for that have I waited that they be prepared to receive that which I have prepared for them -- Ye shall say unto them that which is given unto me of the Father and it shall profit them -- Be ye prepared to receive that which I shall give unto them for them -- And it shall be prepared for thee within the hour - so be it and Beleis---

Beloved of my being: I have prepared a part for them of the Emerald Isle -- And ye may be unto them my hands - and ye shall give unto them that which is given unto me of the Father - and they shall profit thereby - so be it and Beleis ---

Blest of my presence and of the Father which has given unto me that they might receive of Him -- And be ye prepared to go unto them as an Emissary from the place wherein He is -- And ye shall give unto them that which shall be given unto thee of Him -- Ye shall be unto them His hand and His feet - and His mouth -- And ye shall say unto them that which He shall put into thy mouth to say -- And they shall be prepared to receive thee in His Name - and in the Love and mercy which is His ---

Be ye prepared for within the time which is near ye shall stand within the Emerald Isle and ye shall be unto them the lamp which shall be given unto thee of the one and only Sananda - the beloved Son of God the Father - and which they know as the Son of Mary and Joseph of Nazareth -- So be it they shall be prepared to receive thee in His Name - and for their sake shall ye be sent -- And ye shall give unto them as He would have them receive of Him -- And be it so that they shall receive thee in His name and in His love and grace are ye sent ---

And be ye at peace and Poise for ye shall be prepared within the Inner Temple for that which ye are to do -- And ye shall receive thy credentials from the Father which has called thee out from among them in His service - and ye shall be received in His name and in the Light of the Christ -- So be it and Beleis -- Say unto them: Be ye of the Emerald Isle prepared to receive the Emissary which shall be sent out from the Inner Temple of the Father --.for it is come that ye shall be prepared for a new day - for ye shall have a new place of abode -- And ye shall be prepared for that which shall come upon thee -- And it shall profit thee to receive them which are being sent to prepare thee -- For it is given unto this Emissary to be the hands of the Father and Mother made manifest unto thee ---

They shall lift the dead - they shall heal the sick - they shall make the blind to see - and it shall be accomplished according to the law which shall be revealed unto them within the Inner Temple -- And so be it that ye shall receive of the Father's bounty and of the inheritance which He has kept for thee for this time ---

And as ye receive of them which are sent ye receive of the Father -- So be ye prepared - and so be it in the Name of the Most High --

23

I am thy Brother and thy Guardian in the Name of the Host High - and in the service of the Christ -- Marshea -- of the Emerald Cross ---

Blest of my being: Ye shall now receive that which has been prepared for them by our blessed Sister of Light - Nada - for She shall give unto them that which is given unto her of the Father - and it shall be given unto thee in His Name - and so be it and Beleis

**Sister Nada**

Blest of my presence and of my being: I am come unto thee that ye may be my hands unto them which are prepared to receive of that which I am prepared to give unto them - which is given unto me of the Father - Son and Holy Ghost ---

So be it that they shall receive that which is proffered them in love and mercy -- For it is my part to give unto them as I have received - and that which has been my deliverance from bondage -- I have received my inheritance - and I know the joy and freedom from the bonds of Earth and the sorrow which is part of the Earthly inheritance -- I have been given passport unto thee of the Father - that they too may partake of the same joy and freedom ---

And will it not be given unto all to know that which is meant by "Joy and Freedom" -- Yet some shall wait - some shall rush to claim their inheritance - so shall it profit them ---

Why suffer more? When the day of the now dispensation is at hand -- It has been fashioned within the Inner Temple that each and every one might return unto the Father without tasting death -- For

24

that has our blessed Sananda come into the Earth again - to fulfill His mission - and to give unto the children of Earth that which they have not comprehended - that which He demonstrated in the old order which is now passed -- It is the law of the Losolo that one <u>shall learn!</u> and it is come that he shall either learn or be put into the compound wherein he may sleep until he awakens of his own accord ---

It is the day of awakening and yet some shall sleep -- And there shall be a place for them - and they shall not be given quarters within the same place as them which do awake -- And they shall in time become awake - and they too shall be free -- And so be it and Selah ---

Be ye blest of them which have come unto thee that ye may awaken - and that ye may be given that which is fortuned unto thee of the Father - for it is in love and mercy that they come - and for thy sake -- And be ye mindful of them - and give thanks unto the Father that He has sent them - for it shall stand thee in good stead in the time which is near ---

For ye shall turn unto them and ye shall call unto them in thy agony and torment -- And so be ye prepared to be delivered from that which would be unto thee torment -- And as I have given into thee of my love and mercy and wisdom - all shall receive in due time -- So be it and Selah ---

I am thy Sister Nada - and thy servant in the Light of the Christ - and whom ye shall come to know --

Blessings from the Throne of the Father - and the Brothers and Sisters of the Order of the Emerald Cross ---

Blest of my being: Ye shall receive of the one and only Brother Bor - and that which he has kept for them for this time -- And it shall be given unto thee in the Name of the Father - Son and Holy Ghost -- So be it and Beleis ---

## Brother Bor

Blessed one which are my hands unto them: Ye shall now be given my part which I have kept for them -- And it shall be given unto some to receive it - some shall not see it - some shall reject it -- But it is given unto man to have free will - and he shall learn to use it for his own good - and for that which shall profit him and lift up his brothers ---

So be it that I have come that he may learn - and that he may be given in greater capacity -- Be ye as one which can hear that which we thy brothers and sisters are saying unto thee - for ye are now deaf - and blind unto the things which are going on about thee!

It is now time that ye are waking! and that ye stand still - and bear that which is being said -- Be as one which has come into the place wherein ye are to hear that which is being said - that which shall be unto thee of interest - and give unto us thy attention - and ye shall learn many things which ye hitherto have not known -- It is given unto me to be the "Father of discipline"- and ye shall hear much on that - for it shall be given unto thee to know what is meant by discipline ---

Ye of Earth have not been given to discipline - and ye are as untrained children - undisciplined! And ye shall become as adults - and ye shall grow to maturity within a short time -- For the time is now at hand when all shall be as well trained soldiers on the field of duty -- For it is given unto me to know the wisdom of discipline and cooperation -- <u>For now it is one that each and every one shall have a part in the evacuation of the Earth</u> -- And ye shall be called out of thy beds - out of thy places of entertainment - out of thy temples - and ye shall be given instructions beforehand -- And it shall behoove thee to accept them and to remember them!

For sad are they which shall forget -- For in the time which is near ye shall have reason to remember - and so be it and Selah ---

I am come unto thee that ye may be prepared to receive one which shall be sent out from my place of abode as my emissary -- For it shall be given unto them to be the hand and foot of me and of the Father ---

For it is given unto this one to be prepared to prepare thee -- And ye shall be wise to receive them as the emissary which has gone out from my place of abode - and wherein ye shall be received when ye are prepared to enter ---

And so be it that many are sent out from this place to prepare thee -- And ye shall be given an examination ere ye pass the portal of this place wherein I am ---

It is given unto me to wait for thy preparation and I shall come unto thee and sibor thee in the law of the Losoloes which ye shall comprehend and which shall give the mastery over all things -- So be ye prepared to receive my emissary in the Name of the Most High - that ye may be prepared to receive me -- And so be it in the service of the Christ which ye shall come to know ---

I am thy servant and thy Brother in the Name of the most High - Bor - of the Inner Temple - and of the Order of the Emerald Cross -- Recorded by Sister Thedra of the Emerald Cross –

# Part #31

Blest of my being: Ye shall now receive of the one and only Marshea and that which he has prepared for them -- So shall it be given unto them in the Name of the Father - Son and Holy Ghost -- So be it and Beleis ---

## Marshea

Blest of my presence: Ye shall say unto them that which is given unto me of the Father ---

For it is now time that I say unto them which is given unto me to say -- Blest are they which do receive that which the Father would have them receive - for He has willed it that all receive that which is given unto us thy Sibors to give unto them -- Be ye the children of Earth prepared to receive them which shall come unto thee - for they shall be sent from out of the place <u>wherein ye are not prepared to go</u> - and they come that ye may be prepared ---

And for the first time I say unto thee as our blessed Brother Sananda has said - that <u>"There is a place prepared for thee"</u> -- And <u>many shall come unto thee that ye may be brot therein</u> -- And was it not given unto Him to go to prepare a place -- And have ye not waited lo the many centuries for His return?

Now He has returned -- Shall ye not receive Him - and shall ye not awake to His presence - and shall ye not seek Him out? Be ye wise and give unto Him credit - for He has kept His covenant with thee - and it shall profit thee to seek Him out and to call unto Him - - For He knows wherein ye are - and as ye seek Him out He shall be

29

come unto thee in wisdom and prudence -- So be it and Beleis -- I have sat with Him in His secret place of abode ( $\Delta$ $\Delta$ $\Delta$ ) and I have counseled with Him -- And I have received my freedom thru His love and grace -- And as I have received of Him I offer unto thee - for it is given unto me to know the joy and freedom which is our inheritance ---

And be ye of a mind to receive Him and of Him for it is the better part of wisdom -- And as ye receive of us thy Brothers of Light ye have received of the Father -- for we too have received our sonship and are one with the Father -- And for that have we held out a hand unto thee that ye may know the same freedom -- <u>Be ye of a mind to receive the emissaries that are being sent out from the Inner Temple and from the Temple of Osiris</u> - in the Name of the Father - Son and Holy Ghost ---

And so shall they give unto thee that which He has prepared for thee - and that which He would have thee receive of Him -- And so be ye prepared - <u>for thy preparation shall be given in many ways - and at the place wherein ye are -- And so be it that ye shall comprehend that which is being given unto thee</u> - and it shall profit thee -- Be ye alert and see and hear that which is about thee - that which is the sign of the times -- And so shall thy capacity for learning be increased -- So be it and Beleis -- I am thy Brother and thy Sibor - Marshea - Order of the Emerald Cross --

Blest of my being: Ye shall now receive that which is prepared for them by our blessed Brother of Light Romano - and he shall give unto them as he has received of the Father -- So be it and Beleis ---

## Romano

Blest of my being and of my presence: I am come unto thee that they which are so prepared may receive of the Father even as we which have gone the Royal Road ---

So be it that I am come unto thee from the Temple of Osiris and wherein we are prepared to receive them which are prepared to enter -- And wherein is it said: "There are many places prepared to receive them which are brot out of the Earth"? And be ye as one which shall be brot into the place wherein there is light and freedom -- For it has been given unto thee to be bound within the world of darkness - and for this have ye been sad - and have ye known sorrow ---

Say unto the Father: Thy Will be done in me - thru me - by me - and for me -- And thy part shall be given unto thee and ye shall be glad! So be it and Selah ---

We thy Sibors have gained our freedom thru this - and we have received of the Father greater than we knew ---

Was it not given unto us to be the Sons of God the Father - and has He not kept us for this day when each and every one shall know Him -- And be it such as shall free thee from thy bondage - and there shall be great joy and much gladness thruout the realms of Light -- So be it and Beleis ---

Blessed ones of Earth: There are forces of darkness which are built up within thy world which are in wait to destroy thee! and ye have not an iota of conception that which is about thee! and that which ye have created within thy world - and which shall have its wrath -- And ye shall be wise indeed to prepare thyself for the day

31

of reckoning -- For sure as the Sun rises ye shall pay the price for thy wanton and thy folly ---

Yet as ye turn thy face homeward - and call unto the Father for deliverance - He shall send them which are responsible unto Him for thy well-being -- For they have given of themself that they may be prepared to deliver thee -- They have covenanted with the Father that they should not rest until the last one is delivered -- And such is their work - and their promise unto thee -- So be it that they shall keep their word - and they shall fulfill their mission and return unto the father which has sent them unto thee -- So be it and Selah ---

I am one which shall come unto thee from out of the Temple of Osiris and I shall give unto thee of my love and my strength - my knowledge and wisdom that ye may not know sorrow and torment -- And that ye may be made to know thy oneness with the Father and Mother and that ye may return unto them -- Therein ye shall find thy place which has been kept for thee -- <u>Ye have but to reach out and call unto them and ye shall be heard and answered</u> -- We which are sent to sibor thee may say many things unto thee in many ways - and many times -- Yet it is the part of many to say that which shall profit thee and to say it as simply as possible -- For even the child shall be able to comprehend that which we shall say unto thee -- So be it and Selah ---

I am given unto simplicity and therein ye may read within the time which is near that which shall be given unto thee -- For there is but little time that ye have to prepare thyself - and it is but the better part of wisdom to be about thy preparation - and ye shall read as ye run -- For the signs are written upon the stars - within the clouds and within the waters and the sands -- Ye have but to look to see ---

And as ye seek revelation - so shall it be given unto thee -- And I am come unto thee that the fullness of "The plan" shall be revealed unto thee - So be it and Selah -- I am thy Brother and Sibor - in the service of the Christ - and which ye shall come to know -- I am Romano - of the Temple of Osiris - and the Order of the Emerald Cross ---

# Part #32

Blest of my being: Ye shall now prepare thyself to receive of the one and only Beautealu - and that which he has prepared for them -- And it shall be given in the Name of the Father - Son and Holy Ghost -- So be it and Beleis ---

## Beautealu

Blest of my being: It is given unto thee to be my hands unto them - for they shall be blest of the Father which has kept thee for this day -- So shall they receive that which is prepared for them - and which is given unto me of the Father -- So be it that they which receive shall be richly blest -- So be it and Selah ---

Blessed ones which are prepared to receive that which is given unto thee of the Father: I am come unto thee that ye may be prepared to enter into the place wherein He is - that ye may receive thy Sonship - that ye may know that which he has endowed thee -- And will ye not hear me out?

For it is now time that ye become aware of thy Benefactors - and we thy Sibors -- We have waited for this day that ye may receive us -- So be it that we shall become aware of us - for in the time which is near ye shall call unto us and as ye call we shall hear -- Yet ye may be late! - and ye may be given unto torment and discomfort -- While it is yet time ye shall be wise to allow us to come in and counsel thee - and to give thee instructions in thy new part and preparations for thy new place -- And ye shall be glad for knowing us - and ye shall accept us in the Name of the Father - Son and Holy Ghost -- So be it and Beleis ---

Glad ye shall be for being fore-prepared - for it shall stand thee four square - and ye shall be given the fortune to be brot out of the Earth before chaos ---

And therein is wisdom - for sad shall they be which wait! For there shall be chaos - and there shall be cries within the night! I have answered many a cry and I know how sad!

So be ye as wise as the serpent and silent as the sphinx -- And ye shall be lifted up - and ye shall not know sorrow and suffering -- And be ye foretold that there shall be great tidal waves - and there shall be many fires which shall take their toll -- And there shall be winds of great velocity - and they shall blow north and south - and east and west and ye shall not stand against them --

And ye shall remember my words - and ye shall cry: my Lord - my Lord - deliver us! So be ye prepared! ---

As it has been said over again and again: Ye shall remember thy Şibors and ye shall be given that which we have fortuned unto thyself - and as ye have willed it - so be it and Selah -- We which are sent to deliver thee are within thy call -- And we are prepared to give unto thee as ye are prepared to receive -- And so be it and Selah ---

Ye shall not despair for it is given unto us to know thee and to know which is in their heart -- We are not deceived by hollow words ---

And we have waited until ye are prepared to receive us - and we shall reveal ourself unto thee -- So be it and Selah -- And give credit where credit is due - for ye have the key within thy hand unto the

Inner Temple - and ye have but to use it -- So shall it profit thee - and so be it and Selah -- I am thy Older Brother - the Son of the Posied - Beautealu - of the School of the Seven Rays --

Blest of my being: Ye shall now receive of the one and only Posied - and that which he has prepared for them which are to receive of his words -- And they shall be given in the Name of the Father - Son and Holy Ghost -- Amen and Beleis ---

**The Posied**

Blest of my being and of my presence: Be ye as ones which have given unto the Father that ye may receive of Him -- For as ye give so shall ye receive -- And as ye receive of Him so shall ye give unto thy brother - and will ye not profit thereby? For it is come that ye shall be a lamp unto thy brother - and ye shall not be unto him a "poison" -- For ye have not yet learned the wisdom of helping thy brother up - and it is said that "Ye shall be unto him that which we are unto thee" -- Yet ye have not comprehended that which we are to thee! For we have given of ourself that ye may be comforted - and that ye may be healed of thy infirmities - and of thy sickness - and thy blindness -- And that ye may have a capacity for learning - and that ye may grow strong and that ye may know wherein ye are staid -- So be mindful of us and be ye as wise as a serpent - and give unto thy brothers as we thy Sibors give unto thee -- And therein is the greatest of service ---

For it is given unto thee to be the hands and the feet of the Father made manifest upon the Earth - and as ye come to know Him and as ye come to know thyself ye shall hasten to do His bidding -- And shall give thanks unto Him for the privilege of serving thy brother -

and ye shall be glad for thy oneness and for thy knowing -- So be it and Beleis ---

Be ye as a little child and <u>accept</u> that which He proffers thee <u>for it shall be unto thee all things</u> - and ye shall be glad for thy freedom -- And ye shall know as He knows - ye shall be as He - ye shall create even as He creates for ye shall be one with Him -- And ye shall be given thy Sonship and for that have ye waited -- The day is come when all shall be given their choice - and as ye will it - so be it and Selah -- Ye have but to accept it -- And as ye receive of me ye receive of the Father which has sent me - that ye may come to know Him - and ye shall not be deceived - for there are many which have come to bear witness of our being and of that which we say unto them -- So be ye as one which has within thy hand the key to the Inner Temple - ye have but to use it ---

So be of a mind to return unto the Father and Mother from which ye have gone out -- So be it given into thee as ye would have it -- And so be it and Beleis and Selah ---

I am thy Older Brother the Posied - of the Inner Temple - and of the Order of the Emerald Cross ---

Blest of my being: Ye shall now receive of the one and only Osiris - and that which he has prepared for them -- And it shall be given unto thee in the Name of the Father - Son and Holy Ghost -- Amen and Beleis ---

## Osiris

Blessed children of Earth: Wherein is it said that "One" shall be sent out from the Temple of Osiris? And so shall "One" come unto thee as my hands and feet upon the Earth -- Yet it shall - be that "one of thy own" shall be brot into the Temple of Osiris - and they shall be prepared to return unto thee as my emissary - and as a living witness unto thee of that which shall be given unto thee of the Father - Son and Holy Ghost -- So be it that there shall be 'one of our own from this planet' accompany the 'one of Earth' which shall be unto 'that one' sponsor ---

For it is the better part of wisdom that there are two which shall go out together -- And they shall seek out them which are prepared to receive them - and so be it and Selah -- I am come unto thee that ye may be prepared to receive them - and it shall be given unto thee to know them - for they shall be unto thee that which the child of Earth could not be -- And they shall seek thee out and sibor thee in ways which are beyond thy present comprehension -- And so be ye prepared to receive them -- In the Name of the Most High shall they go out from the Temple of Osiris - and they shall be unto thee that which the Father would have them be ---

So be it in the service of the Christ which ye shall come to know -- And ye shall be given that which shall be unto thee thy deliverance from bondage - and ye shall be glad for thy freedom -- So shall ye be prepared to receive them - and as ye receive them ye have received me -- And as ye receive me ye receive the Father - for these which shall go out unto thee shall have received their Sonship even as I - Osiris - and them which have gone the Royal Road -- So be it

38

that ye are foretold and fore-prepared - and it shall be cause for great rejoicing -- So be it and Selah ---

I am thy Older Brother Osiris - of the Temple of Osiris - and of the Order of the Emerald Cross ---

Recorded by Sister Thedra - Order of the Emerald Cross –

# Part #33

Blest of my being: Now ye shall give unto them that which shall be given unto thee of the one and only Michael - and he has given unto thee that which shall be unto thee great revelation -- For he shall say that which he has not said unto thee -- So be ye prepared to receive that which shall be given unto them in the Name of the Father - Son and Holy Ghost -- And so be it and Beleis ---

## Michael

Blessed ones which I have been given and which are offered me of the Father: I have said that "There are none which are out of sight - nor wherein they cannot be found" - and I repeat: "We know our sheep and wherein they are" -- And we know that which is the better pasture - and for that have we been given our part as shepherds for it is given unto us to know that which ye need - and that which shall profit thee -- Was it not said that "Ye shall be moved to greener pasture wherein the waters are fresh and pure"? So be it - and ye shall know the wisdom of that ere it is come that ye are brot out of thy barren land wherein ye have thirsted and hungered -- For it is given unto us thy Guardians to see that which is before thee and thy part which ye shall have -- And it is given unto us to know that which is to come and the consequence thereof ---

Now ye shall give unto me credit for knowing whereof I speak - for long have I been thy pastor - and long have I been within the service of the Christ -- And ye have given little credit unto me -- And forget not that I am responsible for thy well-being and I am

40

given unto patience - and I shall be as one 'seated upon the gate' - and I shall open wide the gate when ye are ready to pass ---

For it is now come that the gate shall open both ways - and as ye are given permission of the Father to enter into the realms wherein we abide - He has given us permission to enter into thy realm - which is the saddest of all realms -- And so be it that ye shall come to know how sad it is!

And for that do we of the realms of Light come that ye may be brot out of thy realm of darkness -- And that ye may know greater freedom - and that ye may come to know the Christ - and so shall it be and Beleis -- I have given of myself that ye may come to know thyself - and that ye may know thy oneness with the Father -- And be ye one which has a will to return unto Him - for from Him have ye gone into the world of sorrow and suffering - and ye have forgotten that which ye once know as thy own home - and that which was thy inheritance ---

It is given unto me to remember thee and that which ye have said unto me before thy sojourn into the Earth -- And I have waited for this day when I might come unto thee -- And when ye shall be given passport into the place wherein I am -- And be ye prepared - for one shall come unto thee from out of my place of abode - and he shall be within this place prepared to give unto thee all that is meant for thee -- And ye shall be given that which ye have prayed for - that which shall deliver thee out of the "barren land" -- And so be it and Selah ---

And will ye not turn homeward and will ye not be received of them which have awaited thy return -- So be it and Selah -- I am thy

41

Pastor and thy Brother in the service of the Christ which ye shall come to know -- So be it and Selah -- Michael of the Sun - and the Order of the Emerald Cross ---

## Sananda

Blest of my being: Ye shall now give unto them that which I shall give unto thee for them -- And it shall serve them well - for it is given in the Name of the Father - Son and Holy Ghost -- Amen and Beleis ---

Beloved ones which are given unto me - and which have been given unto me of the Father: And am I not responsible unto the Father for thee? Have I not given my word that I shall deliver thee out of darkness? And have I not given of myself that it may be done? And will ye not give unto me credit for keeping my covenant with thee? For I said: "I should go to prepare a place for thee" -- And it is done! And I have returned unto thee that ye may be prepared to enter into the place which I prepared for thee -- And yet ye have given little thot unto thy preparation -- As ye have not given credence unto my being - nor have ye given thot of that which is before thee - and that which ye shall become -- So be it that ye shall be reminded of my presence - for I shall give unto thee that which shall suffice thee ---

And ye shall be caught up short - and ye shall be given that which shall remind thee -- And ye shall have reason to seek me out for thy own sake - and ye shall be as one come late -- For it shall behoove thee to seek me early -- And blest are they which seek me early - for they shall be delivered up and they shall know no sorrow and suffering -- And so be ye as one which has prepared thyself to

42

receive of me that ye shall be unto thy brother that which I shall be unto them which are prepared to receive me ---

So be ye as wise as a serpent and silent as sphinx -- And ye shall seek thy salvation within the Father which has sent me unto thee -- And ye shall find thy way into the place wherein He is -- So be it and Beleis -- And so shall I come unto thee in His Name and for His sake -- And be ye as one which can find thy way - and as one which has earned thy passport into the place wherein He is -- And so shall it be given unto many to proffer thee a hand ---

And as ye call out ye shall be heard and answered in love and mercy -- And it is given unto me to know thee - and that which is in thy heart -- And I am not deceived by hollow words - nor am I deceived by the garments ye wear - for they are not part of thee nor of thy preparation -- Ye shall give of thyself and of thy whole self and of thy will unto the Father - And ye shall have cause for rejoicing - and so be it and Beleis -- Many shall come out from the secret place wherein I am and they shall stand ready to groom thee - and they shall be unto thee thy hands and thy feet -- And ye shall give unto them thanks and credit -- For they have come into the world of darkness that ye may be lifted up - that ye may have light - --

And so be it that ye shall give unto me credit for I have opened the way that they may come into thy realm -- And I stand guard at the gate - and I have decreed that none pass which are not of the realms of light -- And so be it that ye shall be mindful of thy benefactors - but for them ye would be sad indeed! And it is given unto me to know how sad!

So be it that ye shall be reminded of them which are responsible for thy well-being -- And so be it and Beleis ---

I am thy Elder Brother -- and thy servant in the Light of the Christ which ye shall come to know -- So be it and Beleis -- Sananda of the Emerald Cross ---

Recorded by Sister Thedra of the Emerald Cross –

# Part #34

Blest of my being: Be ye prepared to receive that which shall be given unto thee in the Name of the Father - Son and Holy Ghost -- So be it and Beleis ---

## Maheru

Beloved of my being: I am thy Sibor and Brother of the School of the Seven Rays which you know as "Maheru" -- And ye shall record my words which shall be given unto them which are ready to receive them -- And ye shall be blest of the Father which has sent me unto thee that they may receive that which I have prepared for them -- So be it that they shall be blest of the Father - Son and Holy Ghost -- Amen and Beleis ---

Say unto them: Be ye blest of the Father - and of the Son and Holy Ghost -- I am come unto thee with that which shall be unto thee much love and wisdom ---

And ye shall search the Scripts which are now given unto thee that ye may be enlightened -- For within them are contained that which shall bless thee eternally -- And it shall be unto thee all that is necessary for thy deliverance from bondage - and therein is thy suffering and sorrow ---

Ye shall seek thy way home - thy return unto thy Source -- And ye shall receive thy Sibors and thy Brothers of Light which have come unto thee out of the realms of Light -- And ye shall receive them in the Name of the Father - Son and Holy Ghost --- Ye have not been schooled in the higher laws of the Losoloes - and ye do not

45

comprehend that which ye are now being given -- Yet the time is near when ye shall - for it is given unto us thy Sibors to be patient - and we shall work with thee that ye may comprehend and that ye may have thy liberation ---

And great shall be our reward! for as one is liberated - ye have no comprehension of the joy and gladness which is released thruout the Father's Kingdom! And it shall be given unto all to know such joy -- For that do we work without ceasing -- And forget not that there is more than tongue or pen can convey unto thee - and no man has ever given unto thee that which ye shall come to know - for it is without words - and within thy own realm of knowledge - and it cannot be conveyed thru words or pen -- It is of the "Arcane" - the unspeakable! And that is the glory of the Father - which ye have been told shall be given unto thee -- And be ye prepared to receive in abundance - for great is His Glory and great is His Mercy and Love -- And will it not be given without stint? for He has endowed all His children with His gifts which ye have but to claim -- And so be it and Beleis ---

I have given of my love - and my strength that this age may come into its fullness - and that ye may find thy way home -- And so be it that my waiting is ended - and my work is not for naught -- And I am within the place wherein I am prepared to receive thee - and ye shall be prepared within the place wherein ye are -- So be it and Beleis -- I am thy Elder Brother and Sibor Maheru - School of the Seven Rays ---

Blest of my being: Ye shall now receive that which is prepared for thee by our blessed Brother of Light - the one and only Ariel --

And that which he has prepared for thee shall be given unto them in the Name of the Father - Son and Holy Ghost -- Amen and Beleis

## Ariel

Blest of my being: Be ye blest of the Father which has sent me unto thee - and ye shall be my hands unto them - and they shall be blest which receive of my words -- For it is given unto me to seek them out which are prepared to receive me -- And so be it that they shall be prepared to receive me in the Name of the Father - Son and Holy Ghost -- And so be it and Selah ---

Blest shall they be which seek me - for I shall come unto them and I shall sibor them - and they shall be given comprehension to know that which I say unto them -- So be it accorded unto them as they will it -- And now I say unto them that there are great revelations awaiting them which shall be the reward of them which seek - and so be it and Selah -- I am prepared to lead them into the secret place wherein they shall see and know - as I know - and I have been prepared within the "Losolo" and within the "Lotus" -- I have been within the Temple of Osiris prepared - and I have passport into the Inner Temple -- So be it that I am prepared to prepare them which present themself ---

And them which are so prepared shall be brot out from among then - and so be it and Selah -- I am one which has come out from the place wherein the Father is and He has given me passport unto thee ---

And He has given unto me as I am prepared to receive - for I have been prepared for this age -- And ye shall come to know me -

and ye shall sit and counsel with me - them which are so prepared - - And so be it in the Name of the Most High ---

And ye shall receive in abundance - and ye shall give unto me credit - for I am one of thy benefactors -- I have given of myself that ye may reach the age of accountability - and that ye may come to know thy oneness with the Father and return unto Him -- And be ye not deceived - for there are many which would turn thee away! <u>And ye shall seek thy salvation within the Father and ye shall keep thy own council - and ask no man for his opinion -- And ye shall be prepared in silence</u> - and ye shall counsel with them which are sent unto thee of the Father - and ye shall be blest of them - for they have come unto thee that ye may know Him -- And so be it and Beleis Selah

I am thy Older Brother and Sibor Ariel of the Temple of Osiris and the Order of the Emerald Cross ---

Blest of my being: Ye may now receive of one which ye know as Aumen - and that which he has prepared for thee -- And it shall be given unto them which are prepared to receive that which he has prepared for them -- So be it given unto thee in the Name of the Father - Son and Holy Ghost -- Amen and Beleis ---

## Aumen

Blest of my being and of my presence: I am come unto thee out of my place of abode - and for the purpose of adding my light unto that of my brothers and sisters - that ye may come to know that which hither to has been kept secret from the uninitiated - and will ye too not be initiated? And will ye not too be found worthy to receive that which shall be revealed unto thee? <u>For none pass within the gates</u> <u>which are found wanting</u> -- So be it that ye shall be prepared to enter into the Temple of the Most High -- And ye shall be glad for thy preparation -- And so be it and Selah -- I am one which has watched thy progress lo the eons of thy Earthly journey -- And I have been unto thee pastor - and Sibor -- And I have gone into the shadows with thee ---

I have found my way home - even as ye too shall -- I know the human frailties - and I know wherein thy strength lies - for I have been given that which is now proffered unto thee -- And I shall stand ready to bring thee out into the place wherein I am when ye are prepared -- And so be it that I shall await thy call - and ye shall be given as ye are capable of receiving -- <u>So be it that many await thy</u> <u>call -- For as the call has gone out thru the Cosmos have we</u> <u>answered -- And as we thy guardians - thy Sibors - thy benefactors</u> <u>- call unto thee - shall ye respond in haste - and wisdom ---</u>

For the time is nigh upon thee that ye shall come to know that which is come unto thee - and it shall be given unto thee to know much sorrow and suffering in the day ahead -- And we thy Sibors have given unto thee that which should suffice thee -- For it is come that ye shall be alerted from every place within the Earth -- <u>And ye</u> <u>shall be given warning - and time to prepare thyself -- Yet time shall</u> <u>run out! and ye shall be wise indeed to begin the preparation this day</u> - for ye are not promised tomorrow! And be ye as one that can heed the warning and make haste that ye shall not be found wanting! ---

So be it that the Father which has sent us unto thee shall give unto thee as He has given unto us of His bounty - and His Grace and Mercy -- <u>So be ye as wise as a serpent and silent as a sphinx</u> - and be ye prepared to receive that which is kept for thee -- And ye shall be richly blest -- And so be it and Beleis ---

Be ye as one which can stand within the Light of the Christ made whole - and ye shall come to know that which is the Christ -- And so be it and Beleis -- Selah -- And give unto the Father credit for thy being and call unto Him -- And as ye receive of Him so shall ye receive us - thy Brothers of Light and thy Sibors -- Ye shall be lifted up in His Name - and of His Grace and Mercy shall ye partake -- And so be it and Selah ---

I am thy Brother and Sibor in the service of the Christ - and of the Emerald Cross - Aumen ---

Recorded by Sister Thedra of the Order of the Emerald Cross --

# Part #35

Blest of my being: Be ye prepared to receive of the one which ye know as sister Saboni, and that which she has prepared for 'them.' For she has gone the long way to bless them and now she gives unto them of her love and mercy that they may come to know the Father as she knows him, so be it and Beleis.

## Sister Saboni
### Guardian of Italy

Blessed one, which I shall ask to be my hand unto them, will ye not partake of my love, and my grace, which is given unto me of the Mother Sara, for I am within the place wherein she is. And she has given unto me of herself that I may bless thee. And so be it and Beleis and Selah.

I am come that they which are within the place wherein I have labored for many years shall become aware of that which is offered unto them at this time. And that which has been promised them from the beginning of her history.

Is it not said that our Blessed Master shall return? And was it not given unto him to go into the place wherein the Father is, and to receive his son ship? And did he not return unto them and give of himself that they should receive of the Father as he? And did they hear him? And did they not slay him because of their unbelief? And has not the saints been martyred lo the many centuries?

Yet we are promised that "the day of martyrdom is passed" and the workers in the light of the Christ shall be free to do the work of the Father, and so be it and Selah. I have given of myself that this day may come that the servants of the Father may be free, and so shall there be great joy and much gladness. For it is sad indeed that they have been given to such sacrifice.

And the day is come when they shall stone for their sacrifice of blood. And ye shall say unto them that the day of Blood is past; the day of light is come! And they shall remove the blood from their alters! and they shall clean them! and they shall replace their idols with the lamps which shall be given unto them. And their alters shall be bright and shining: they shall no longer pray unto the parish, they shall call unto the Father the cause of their being - and they shall give unto Him the glory and praise for their being: and yet they shall give unto him credit for sending them when He has sent out in His name unto them that they too shall be brought into the place which is prepared for them.

And is it not written and wisely so, that the old order is ended, and the day of the new dispensation is come? So be it and Selah. And was it not given unto me to serve in the temples of the lotus, and within the temples and the schools of the land of Italy, and have I not known the darkness of the 'old order,' have I not served to the best of my ability that they may be brought out of darkness? Have I not cried unto the Father, Light, More Light! that I might be a lamp unto their feet? Have I not gone the long way to bless them? And am I not glad for the new dispensation wherein they may receive their inheritance?

Have ye too not served according to thy ability? and shall ye not be better for thy effort? And shall ye not be rewarded for thy waiting? So be it and Selah.

I say unto my country men, be ye prepared for that which shall come upon thee. For great shall be thy suffering and sorrow. And for that shall one be sent that ye may be brought out before the day of chaos, that we may not know suffering and sorrow. So be ye prepared to receive them in the name of the Father which has called them: and as he has called so have they answered him.

And they shall be sent unto thee in His name and in the service of the Christ, which ye shall come to know. So be it and Selah.

I am thy servant in the service of the Most High, and of the Order of the Emerald Cross. I am thy Sister Saboni.

Blest of my being: Be ye at Peace and Poise, and ye shall receive of the one and only Beautealu and that which he has prepared for 'them.' And ye shall give it unto them in the name of the Father, Son, and the Holy Ghost; amen and Beleis.

## Beautealu

Blest of my being: and of my presence, for I am come unto thee that ye may receive of the Father, even as I receive of Him, and that ye shall be blest of Him even as I am blest of Him, so be it and Selah.

Be ye as the hands of me made manifest unto them, for as I shall receive of the Father, shall I give unto thee. And as ye receive of me ye have received of the Father that they which are prepared may receive that which is their inheritance, so be it and Selah.

And give unto them these words, that they may be prepared to receive me in the name of the Father, Son and the Holy Ghost. For in the time which is near I shall go into the 'World of Men' and I shall give unto them that which is given unto me of the Father, and it shall profit them to be prepared to receive me. And as it is given unto me to know them I shall seek them out, and I shall give unto them as they are prepared to receive. For it is the better part of wisdom that I reveal myself unto them. For it is now come that many shall reveal themself.

And so be it that the beloved Sananda, and the blessed Posied, shall be among them. And they shall become aware of their presence for it is given unto them to go out among them. And as ye are prepared to receive them so shall they reveal themself. So shall it profit thee to prepare thy self to receive them, for there shall be great joy and much gladness within the place wherein ye shall be brought them which are so prepared to partake of this joy and gladness. And be ye of a mind to receive that which has been kept for thee for it shall be thy deliverance. And so be it and Beleis,

I am within the place wherein the Blessed Posied and our blessed brother of Light, Sananda are, and they have given of themself that ye may be prepared for this day when ye shall stand free, and when ye shall receive thy 'sonship' even as they, and ye shall come to know them and the part ye have had with them. And so be it and Selah.

I am given unto preachments, and I shall say again and again that it shall behoove thee to be up and about thy preparation, and it shall provide thee much light and wisdom.

And as ye have no concept of that which is in store for thee ye shall be wise to trust thy Sibors and to heed that which they say unto thee; and it shall stand thee four square. It shall be unto thee thy deliverance from bondage. And ye shall be glad for thy deliverance, so be it and Beleis. Before thee is the plan of thy salvation: and shall ye be so foolish as to reject it: and shall ye be as the "one which has thrown thy life belt over board?" And <u>I say give unto the Father credit for thy being and give unto Him thy whole self, thy heart, thy will and thy hands, and ye shall be blest of Him, and He shall send unto thee them which shall deliver thee:</u> so be it, and be ye of a mind to receive of Him, and for that have I come that ye may know Him and that ye may return unto Him. And so be it and Selah.

I am thy older brother and Sibor, Beautealu, son of the Posied, and of the School of the Seven Rays.

Blest of my being: ye shall now receive of the Posied and which he has for 'them,' and it shall be given unto them of the Father, Son and Holy Ghost, so be it and Beleis.

**The Posied**

Blest of my being and of my presence: I am come as my son Beautealu, and that they may have more Light and a greater capacity for learning. And that they may alert themself and return unto the Father and that they may know wherein they are staid, so be it and Selah. And as it is given unto me to know where of I speak I shall say unto them again that I have come unto them that they may be prepared for a new place of abode. And their place is prepared for them, and they shall be prepared for it, and therein is wisdom.

Forget not that which has been said unto thee, for it is said for a purpose and said simply and wisely and in few words. And as yet ye are as ones with stiff necks have not turned thy face, nor have ye bowed thy head. And ye have not said that which we have waited to hear. And as ye are given unto idolatry ye shall be brought to account for thy idolatry. And ye shall be given as ye portion out for thyself and it shall be given unto thee measure for measure. And as ye are prepared to receive of we thy Sibors so shall we come in and Sibor thee. And we shall give unto thee in love and wisdom. And ye shall profit much to receive us in the name of the Father, Son and Holy Ghost. So be it that ye shall have that which is fortuned unto thee of the Father, and ye shall be glad the day of thy deliverance is come.

And so be it that ye shall be given thy inheritance and ye shall be one with the Father/Mother which has sent thee out, and ye shall return into them purified even as ye went out, and so be it and Selah.

I am thy older brother and Sibor of the Order of the Emerald Cross, The Posied.

# Part #36

Blest of my being: Be ye prepared to receive that which shall be given unto thee of the one and only Brother Bor, and that which he has for them. So be it given unto thee in the name of the Father, Son and Holy Ghost, amen and Beleis.

## Brother Bor

Blest one: which shall be unto 'them' my hands and my feet: Give unto them these words which shall be given of the Father, that they may receive that which is prepared for them. And it shall profit them. And ye shall be blest: and give unto them that which is said unto thee. And they shall be reminded that there are none so small and none so great that they do not receive of the blessings which are sent out from the throne of the Father/Mother. For as ye serve as my hands unto them they which are on the altar of the inner temple give unto thee as ye sent out. And as ye give ye receive. And as ye give of thy self that they may receive, so do we replenish thee.

And as thy cup is emptied so do we fill it to overflowing. And so be it that the Father has provided that ye shall be fed and nourished, and that ye shall not want: nor shall ye know sorrow. For ye have answered the call. And as ye have been given assignments ye have responded with love, and with haste. And so be it that ye shall be greatly blest.

And within the time which is near ye shall give unto them a 'new part' which shall be given unto thee within the place wherein <u>I am</u>. And they shall partake of thy wisdom, and of thy grace, and they shall know that which is given unto them is from the inner temple.

And they shall not deny thee, nor that which is given unto them. And so be it that ye shall be as my hands and my feet, for I shall summons thee and ye shall respond in haste. And I shall give unto thee that which I have prepared for thee: and ye shall stand before the twenty four elders and ye shall receive of each that which they have for thee. And ye shall return as the emissary unto them. And ye shall say unto them that which is given unto thee of the Father to say: and they shall listen and comprehend that which ye say unto them.

For as ye are prepared to return unto them they shall be prepared to receive thee, so be it and Selah. I say unto them that there shall be one sent out from the place wherein I am, and they shall receive them in the name of the Father, Son and Holy Ghost. And so be it that they shall be greatly blest, and they shall be glad for their preparation. So be it and Beleis. Be ye alert and watchful, and give thanks unto the Father that this day is come, and the day of the new dispensation when everyone may have passport unto the place wherein I am. And so be it and Selah.

I am thy Brother Bor, of the Order of the Emerald Cross and the Temple of Osiris.

Blest of my being: Ye shall now receive that which is prepared for thee by the one and only Osiris, and it shall be given unto them which are prepared to receive of that which he has prepared, so be it given unto thee in the name of the Father, Son, and Holy Ghost, amen and Beleis.

## Osiris

Blest of my presence: and of my being: I am come unto thee that ye may be prepared for that which shall be given unto thee, that they may receive through thee that which the Father has for them. For it is given unto the child of earth to be as the "Thomases" which have to see to believe, and it shall be given unto them to "see" for they shall be touched and they shall be made to see! And so be ye prepared for a new part which ye shall give unto them in the name of the Father, Son and Holy Ghost. So be it that it shall profit them. And ye shall go unto them and ye shall give unto them that which shall be given unto thee for them, <u>for it is so decreed that they shall have proof of that which we the Sibors have</u> said.

And they shall be brought out of their stupor for they shall alert themself and they shall be as ones prepared. And wherein is it said that "they shall go in a prepared people,"

And so shall they and for that has many been sent that they be alert and prepared. Now it is come that there shall be much action and they shall be given that which they can comprehend. And they which do not stir shall be moved (taken away) and they shall be as ones which have betrayed themself. And so be it that they shall be put into a place separate and apart from the rest, and they shall be as ones which have not awakened. So be it and Beleis. Blest are they which do awaken for they shall see God the Father. And they shall receive their inheritance, so be it and Selah.

Ye shall say unto them that ye have received thy inheritance in full, and that ye know the Father, and that he have concourse into his place of abode, and so be it and Selah. And ye may be prepared so that ye may prepare them, and so be it and Selah.

I am come that all may be prepared to receive their inheritance, and yet some shall reject it, and many shall receive it. And them which do receive it shall be prepared to give unto their fellows they brothers in like manner. So be it and Beleis. And there shall be great rejoicing throughout the Father's realm, so be it and Selah.

I am thy Sibor, and elder brother of the temple of Osiris and of the Emerald Cross, Osiris.

Blest of my being: Be ye prepared to receive that which is prepared for thee by the one and only Aumen, for he has prepared a part for them in the name of the Father Son and Holy Ghost. Amen and Beleis.

## Aumen

Beloved, which shall give unto them of thy self that they may receive these words of mine: and for that shall ye receive of the Father which has sent me unto thee that they might receive of Him, so be it and Beleis. Be ye as one which knows wherein ye are staid, and from whence cometh thy help. And so be it and Beleis.

Say unto them that I am among them and that I am given the part which shall be unto them comfort: And I shall guard their liberty with the 'life' which the Father has endowed me. And that I am in my place prepared to defend it, for it is given unto me to be sent out from the temple of liberty, and I am given to much preparation.

And I say unto them "BE YE NOT FEARFUL" - for there are many which stand guard, and not a poultice are we, for we use no poultices. We are given to complete that which we begin. And ye shall be given the protection which ye (Americans) have inherited from the founders of thy Republic! and ye shall be unto her loyal. And ye shall not be given unto hatred for therein is folly, for it shall be the better part of wisdom to love the wanton children: and they shall see thy Light and return unto their rightful place.

So be ye of a mind to partake of the flame of liberty, and the love which enfolds it. And ye shall be as a lamp unto their feet. And ye shall be given thy place upon the alter. And ye shall hold high the "lamp of freedom." And ye shall have no weapons other than that which is the "sword of light and truth." And ye shall not teach thy children hatred, for it is but the chains which shall bind thee!

<u>Ye shall be glad for thy preparation for the day is neigh when all men shall sit and council with me as brothers</u>. And they shall be as ones which have laid aside their weapons of the old order. And they shall clasp hands as brothers: and they shall sing praises unto the Father for their preparation, for it shall be a day of thanksgiving and a day of great joy! when all men shall receive their freedom.

And for that have I worked without ceasing for many centuries. And ye shall come to know me, and ye shall sit in council with me, and ye shall receive that which ye are prepared to receive. So be it that the flame of freedom shall burn upon all the alters of the earth, and there shall be great rejoicing throughout the earth! So be it in the name of the most high and in the light of the Christ which ye shall come to know. And so be it and Selah.

I am thy sibor, and thy guardian of Liberty, and thy older brother of the Emerald Cross and of the Brotherhood of the Seven Rays, Aumen* (St. Germain).

Blest of my being: Ye shall now give unto 'them' that which our blessed Sister of Light, Mura, has prepared for them. And it shall be given unto them in the name of the Father, Son and Holy Ghost. So be it and Beleis.

## Mura

Blessed sister of the Emerald Cross: Ye shall be unto me my hands and my mouth unto them. For ye shall speak unto them as the Father would speak unto them. And it is given unto me to be thy contact unto Him for this part which I shall give unto thee for them which are prepared to receive of my words and that which is given unto me of the Father. So be it that they too shall receive of Him.

*Yes, ye shall say unto them that this one which ye know as Aumen is one and the same as the one known as Saint Germain. Aumen and I are one and the same.

# Part #37

Blest of my being: ye shall now receive of me and that which I have for thee, and ye shall give it unto them in the name of the Father, Son and Holy Ghost. So be it and Beleis.

Say unto them that there are many which shall come out from the inner temple and that they shall be given unto as they are prepared to receive. And as I have recounted unto thee in the beginning of thy ministry that I too was given an initiation into the inner temple at the age of thirteen. And at that time I was an outcast of a temple of Egypt where my mother had taken me, and wherein I was rejected because I was a "non-conformist" and wherein they served the black dragon. And I said, "this is not my place - not for me!" and I wandered into the sands of the desert in search of - I knew not what? - and I reclined upon the sands within the shadow of the sphinx and in a short time I was a boat land nearby and as I knew nothing else I exclaimed as I arose to my feet, "What is this - a boat upon the sand as dry as ash?" And the one within stepped forward and greeted me saying, "My son, we need no water, for this boat cometh unto the earth even as the beams of light.

And lest ye be of the wrong opinion, come with me, and I shall show thee that which shall serve thee well." And I stepped forth into the boat and she sailed out beyond the planet Caldon, and on to the planet Venus, where upon I received instructions in the inner temple. I stood before the throne of the Father, and before the twenty four elders and there I received my 'sonship' and my passport unto the Father. And in the time which I was there I was prepared to return into the earth and to give unto them that which I had received.

And when it was given unto me to return I made straight way unto the temple to report that which had been given unto me to learn - and as the priesthood (as today) would not receive me nor that which I brought unto them, they sat about to discredit me and the message of the Father! and it was given unto me to wander over the earth and to give unto them which were capable of comprehending that which I had received in the inner temple. And it was done in secret, and in wisdom, for there were many which were determined that the message which I brought should not be spread!

And I gave unto them in secret code - and in veiled terms that which the priesthood could not decipher. And they sat about to seize me and to end my mission. And as the Father had so prepared me, and foretold me of that which should come upon me, I sat about to record my experiences and that which I had learned. And to this day they have not fallen into the hands of the priesthood!

And they are carefully secreted within the secret place - and wherein they shall remain for the enlightenment of them of the new order. And therein are letters from and to my beloved mother, and it shall be given unto her to be present when the seal is broken, and we shall share the joy of this day together. So be it and Beleis.

And it shall be given unto many to read the records and to know that which I say to be valid. And ye which are so prepared may enter into the secret places and read for thy self. And so be it and Beleis. I have given unto thee in part and ye which are so prepared shall receive in full. So be it and Beleis.

I am thy elder brother and sibor of the temple of Osiris, The Order of the Emerald Cross and of the inner temple, and in the service of the Christ which ye shall come to know. Sananda, Son of God and of Mary and Joseph of Nazareth.

Blest of my being: Ye shall now be prepared to receive the one and only Coro, and ye shall give into them that which he has prepared for 'them' for it shall be given unto them to receive much from him in the name of the Father, Son and Holy Ghost. Amen and Beleis.

## Coro

Blest of my presence, and of the Father which has given me passport unto thee. And will ye not receive of Him of thy own account? And such is thy inheritance: and so be it and Beleis.

I am come unto thee that ye may give unto them which are prepared to receive that which I have for them. And them which are given to searching the scripts and they which have sought that which is recorded upon the parchments, and upon the stones of earth shall profit to heed that which I say; for it is the better part of wisdom to hear me out: and to follow that which is said unto them. It is given unto them in "parts" for a reason and wisely so! and so be it that they which are so prepared may comprehend the wisdom thereof.

And so shall they which follow, and which heed that which has been said here to fore shall be given much which shall serve to enlighten them. They shall be brought into the secret places and they shall see that which has been hidden from the eyes of the is profane. They shall stand in awe of the wonders of the earth, and they shall be as "little children in wonderland." And they shall wonder at the glory and beauty and at the place wherein they shall go. For it is given unto me to know: for I have seen them weep with joy, and appreciation of the beauty and glory! I have seen them kiss the earth on which they stood in gratitude. For I have given them of my strength that they might move themself - for they have stood prostrate before the grand portal which leads into the inner chambers. For not any figment of thy imagination can convey unto thee that which is hidden within the vortex of the earth! and that which is sealed shall be unsealed for the initiate which is so prepared to enter. And wherein is it said that "none shall enter unprepared?" So be it and Selah.

I am come unto thee that ye may be prepared to enter. Therein is great revelation and great wisdom. And it shall be given unto some to enter therein, and they shall give unto thee in part and in wisdom that which they have seen and learned: Yet it shall not suffice thee; for to see is to know! And so be it that some shall bear witness of my words, and they shall be unto thee my hands and my feet, for I am in the place wherein I am prepared to receive them which are prepared to enter, and so be it and Selah.

I am the keeper of the secrets in the place wherein ye shall go, and so be it that ye may be prepared to enter therein: <u>Ye have but to apply thy self, and seek me out, and I shall give unto thee that which ye are prepared to receive.</u>

I am thy older brother of the Temple of Osiris: and of the Emerald Cross. I serve in the light of the Christ, and so be it ye may come to know that which is the Christ. I am Coro.

Blest of my being: Ye shall now receive that which is prepared for thee by the one and only Esmeraldo, which has given of himself

66

that this may be brought about. He has worked with the ones which has gone before thee. And he has given of his love and of his wisdom that ye shall come to know that which goes on about thee. He has given unto us much without recognition and without stint. He has gone into the fields of battle; he has brought out them which have been wounded; he has stood sponsor for them at the karmic board. He has given of himself that they may return to their loved ones and that they may complete that for which they come into embodiment, and that they might give unto others as they have received. And he has gone into the homes of them wherein the ones in despair were found and he has given unto the comfort and hope.

He has gone into the places wherein the helpless lay and he has given them strength and hope. He has brought them out of the ships aflame. And they have been given that which he has portioned out of his own, that they may walk end see, and that they may be restored, and they have not remembered him.

And so be it that they shall come to know him, and so be it and Beleis. And be ye prepared for he shall come unto thee and he shall prepare thee for a new part. And so be it and Beleis.

**Esmeraldo**

Blest one which I know so well: be ye blest of my presence, and of the Father, I am one which has stood sponsor for thee, and ye have but little knowledge of me. I have given unto thee of my strength that ye may go into the places wherein ye have been; and I have given unto thee power to begin thy new day. I have given unto thee when ye have wept with pain. I have given unto thee patience which has enabled thee to go ahead. And the grand achievement which has been brought about through the cooperation of the two has been cause for much rejoicing.

And so shall ye come to know me and ye shall be unto me grateful for that which ye have received of me. For it is now come that them which I have sponsored shall be "called into action," for it is the day of action! And they shall be brought into the place wherein they shall receive instructions for their new parts, and they shall be as 'soldiers on the field of duty."

They shall present themself fit and ready for duty. And they shall be given that which is sufficient unto the, and unto their new parts and they shall give of themself that the Fathers work may be done through them. And for that have I sponsored them.

And it shall be given unto each to remember me, and the part which they have had with me.

And they shall be unbound and they shall see and hear, and they shall comprehend that which they see and hear. And so be it and Selah. And they shall give unto the Father credit for their being and they shall give unto me credit for their recovery, and for their well-being; so shall they grow in strength and wisdom, and so be it in the name of the father, and Son and Holy Ghost. I am thy Sibor and thy brother in the service of the Christ and of the School of the Seven Rays and of the Temple of Osiris. I am Esmeraldo. Recorded by Sister Thedra of the Emerald Cross and the School of the Seven Rays.

# Part #38

Blest of my being: Be ye prepared to receive the one and only Beautealu, and that which he has prepared for 'them,' and it shall be given unto them in the name of the Father, Son and Holy Ghost. Amen and Beleis.

## Beautealu

Blest of my being, and of my presence: I come unto thee that ye may receive of the Father that which he would have them receive. <u>And it is given unto me to say unto them that there shall be much activity within the "world of men - and inter planetary" for there shall be many which shall be put into new places, and as they are prepared so shall they be given their new places and their assignments.</u>

And it is the better part of wisdom to be prepared! For it will is given unto everyone to be removed from the surface of the earth within the time which is near.

And ye shall be given thy place as ye are prepared to fill it. And so be it that there shall be great changes, and the earth shall undergo many changes, and there shall be much suffering and sorrow. And ye shall be wise to hear that which has been said unto thee.

Ye shall have no fear, for ye shall be given that which has been promised unto thee. Ye shall be delivered up and ye shall not know suffering, if ye are so prepared! There is wisdom in being prepared! and forewarned. (For it is a sad part to be caught unprepared.)

And ye shall not be panicked, for panic is the most sad of all, and none shall panic which are prepared; for ye shall be as well trained soldiers; ye shall be within thy place prepared. And ye shall be made to hear that which shall be said unto thee. Ye shall be prepared to give comfort unto them about thee; and ye shall say unto them that which shall be said unto thee. Ye shall be prepared to give comfort unto them about thee, and ye shall say unto them that which shall be given unto thee of the Father: for ye shall be quickened unto that which he shall say unto thee.

And ye shall give unto them within thy charge, them within thy care, instructions as we thy Sibors shall give unto thee. And ye shall prepare them that they shall not be fearful. So be it that ye shall be lifted up as the lamb is lifted up by the condor. And ye shall be in thy place as a beacon of light; <u>for as ye are calm and at peace and poise shall we find thee</u> - <u>and ye shall be brought out before chaos</u>! And so be it that I have given of myself that ye shall not have any panic nor suffering. So be it that ye shall give unto them which are unto that end credit, and ye shall give unto them thy cooperation, and there shall be order; for out of chaos shall come order. And be ye as my hands and my feet, for as I have been prepared I am prepared to prepare thee. And so shall I do my utmost to bring thee out before ye shall have any sorrow or torment.

And so be it that many are sent to deliver thee out of thy bondage and of thy darkness, so be it and Beleis. I am thy older brother, and thy sibor and thy servant, in the Light of the Christ, which ye shall come to know. I am Beautealu, of the school or the Seven Rays.

Blest of my being: Ye shall now receive that which is prepared for 'them' by our blessed brother of light, O, known unto thee as

Maroni, and he shall give unto thee that which is given unto him of the Father, so be it and Beleis.

**Maroni**

Blest of my presence and of my being: I am come unto thee that ye may receive that which is given unto me to say. For it is my part to groom them which present themself for preparation and entrance into the inner temple. And be it so that I have worked for a long time that each and every one may be delivered out of bondage. And that they may stand free, and that they may receive their inheritance of the Father.

And now it is come, and as the Father has given me passport into the world of men I shall give unto thee that which he has given unto me for thee. We each have a part for thee. And it is my part to groom thee for thy entrance. And ye shall be given that which shall be unto thee profitable.

For it is given unto me to know wherein ye are lacking. I shall give unto thee that ye may be strengthened in thy weak parts. So be it and Selah.

I am given unto patience and I shall wait, and as ye are prepared to receive me I shall come unto thee and I shall give as ye are prepared to receive. And be ye blest of the presence of them which have reached out a hand that ye may be prepared: for it is the greatest of service! And ye shall come to know the great activity which goes on behind the veil, and it shall be parted that ye may step through, even as we have stepped through into thy world of darkness. And ye shall know as we know - and ye shall walk with us thy Sibors and

71

brothers of Light. And be ye so prepared that ye may receive us. In Love, Mercy and Wisdom has the Father sent us unto thee. And there are many on the threshold of thy world ready to receive thee and to be unto thee comfort, and ready to deliver thee up, and so be it and Beleis.

I have worked without ceasing for the day when ye shall be delivered. For in the time to come ye shall know the effort which has been given unto this project which is now coming to maturity. And ye shall stand in awe of the cooperation and love which has been given unto the children of earth, for we have foreseen that which ye have inherited, and that which shall be given unto thee. And we are given to preparation, for it is our port to be prepared for such that which we now are to do for thee, and to be prepared for any event which may call for our service and attention. So be it that ye shall come to know as we thy Sibors now, and to be prepared for that which shall be given unto thee to do.

So be it in the name of the Most High. I am thy servant, and thy brother in the Order of the Emerald Cross and the Brotherhood of the Seven Rays. I am known as Maroni.

Blest of my being: Ye shall now receive of the blessed Sister of Light, Nada, which has prepared a part for 'them,' and they shall receive it in the name of the Father, Son and Holy Ghost. So be it and Beleis.

**Sister Nada**

Blessed Sister, which shall be my hands made manifest unto them: Be ye blest of my presence and of the Father. And it is come that ye

72

shall have thy new part, and ye shall come to know me even as I know thee, and so be it and Beleis.

I am come that each and every one which so "wills" it may be brought into the inner temple: and that they may receive that which is their inheritance, so be it that it is offered unto them. And shall it not be given unto them this day of light when they have but to accept it. And such is the plan which has been given unto thee of the new dispensation. Could ye but see as we see and know as we know that which has been kept for thee and the joy and gladness which ye have inherited ye would be prostrate before the gate of freedom. And ye would be crying for deliverance. And yet ye do not know how sad is thy part: for it is given unto thee to be bound and ye see not beyond thy own limited horizon. And in the time which is near ye shall be given a new part and ye shall be called to account for every idle word and deed which is not inspired by the Christ. And ye shall call unto us for deliverance and mercy. And ye shall be in the "Blackness of Night," for ye cannot say how long ye shall wait to be delivered. And it shall profit thee to seek the light while it is yet time, for it is said, "Blest are they which seek the Father early." And so be it and Beleis.

Be ye in thy place prepared for that which shall be given unto thee, for it shall be given unto thee to experience many new things - many things which shall seem strange unto thee. Yet it shall profit thee to be alert and watchful, for it is given unto thee that ye may be reminded of thy source, and that ye may be prepared to return unto it, the Father and Mother, from which ye have gone out. And so be it and Selah. Blest are they which give of themself that the brother may be lifted up - and be ye reminded of them which have proffered thee a hand: that ye may be lifted up; and forget not that ye have been kept for this day that ye may have free communication into the inner temple, and that ye may know the Father, and Mother. And be it such as is our mission that everyone know that which we know. And therein shall be thy salvation and thy deliverance. So be it and Beleis.

Blest are they which have gone the royal road; and blest shall ye be to receive them in the name of the Father, son and Holy Ghost. Amen and Selah.

I am thy Sister Nada, of the Order of the Emerald Cross, and of the Inner Temple. So be ye prepared to enter in.

Blest of my being: be ye prepared to receive that which is prepared for them by the one and only Michael, and it shall be given unto thee in the name of the Father, Son and Holy Ghost. So be it and Beleis.

## Michael

Beloved one: Ye shall give unto them these words that they may remember wherein they are staid. And they shall be reminded of me when they are called to task, for I am the One given to preachments. I am alert and watchful, and I know that which is given unto them of the Father, and that which they fortune unto themself. <u>And it is sad indeed to see them grovel within the swines burrow, when they are the sons of the living God. And they have forgotten that which they are heir to.</u> So shall they be reminded again and again. And they shall be called one by one. And they shall be brought to account for their wanton - and for their idolatry - and they call themself

74

Christians! And they set themself up as the example of the Christ, and they know not what is meant by the Christ. And they cry Anti Christ! when they do not know what they say. And so be it that they shall give an accounting, and they shall be given as they have given unto their brothers.

And now I shall give unto them of my love, and of my wisdom. Yet they shall be made to know what is meant by discipline! And it is given unto me to carry the flaming sword of Light, and I shall use it, and they shall remember me, Michael, their shepherd, and one which is not asleep, for it is given unto me to be wakeful and watchful.

And I shall be unto them that which shall serve them well. And ye shall give unto them these words, and they shall see that which Michael has said unto them, and they shall take them for what they are worth, for I have said them for each and every one who reads. And be it for a purpose which shall serve its purpose. And as they are mindful of me so shall they be mindful of the Father which has sent me; and be it such as shall profit them, for now it is come that they shall be gathered in, and they shall be given a new part. And they shall be given a number, and they shall answer when it is called, for it shall be given unto them to know their number. And they shall be sad indeed if they have not heard, and if they do not answer. For it is given unto me to know, for I have been within the place wherein the plan is revealed. And it is given unto many to send out the call, and many are sent to find them and to bring them in. So be it and Selah.

I am one which has kept a part for them and it is ready; and as they are ready so shall they receive it, and so be it such as shall profit

75

them. I am in the place wherein I am prepared to receive them which are prepared to enter in; and so be it and Selah.

Be ye blest of my presence and receive of my peace and poise, for I am thy Sibor and thy Brother in the Temple of Osiris and of the Emerald Cross. I am thy shepherd Michael. Recorded by Sister Thedra of the Emerald Cross and the Brotherhood of the Seven Rays.

# Part #39

Blest of my being: Be ye prepared to receive that which is prepared for thee by the one and only Grand Master, and that which he has prepared for 'them' and so shall it be given unto thee in the name of the Father, Son and Holy Ghost. Amen and Beleis.

## Most Worthy Grand Master

Be ye blest of me and be ye blest of them which come unto thee that 'they' receive of us, and that 'they' may learn that which is fortuned unto 'them' of the Father/Mother which has sent them out. And so be it that I shall give unto 'them' which are prepared to receive me. For in the time which is near 'they' shall be given a part which is new unto 'them,' and 'they' shall have need of instructions from the inner temple. And I stand ready to be the instructor. I have waited for this day when 'they' may prepare themself to enter into the place wherein I am. And so be it that the day is come when many shall stand before the throne of the most High Living God, and they shall receive their 'sonship' and they shall be free! even as the ones which have not gone out from the Father/Mother, and they shall have their inheritance in full. So be it and Selah.

I am come unto thee that ye may be unto them my hands made manifest and that they may know me, and that they may be reminded of them which hold them fast. And them which are so minded shall be brought in - in this day, and therein shall be great cause for rejoicing! And they shall be glad, so be it, and Selah. I am of a mind to give unto each and every one the fortune I have kept for them,

77

and they have but to apply themself and to be prepared to receive it, and so shall it be given in love, mercy and wisdom.

For the first time I say unto them that there shall be <u>one</u> go out from the inner temple and they shall be as one which has received their sonship, and they shall be unto 'them' that which I am, and that which the Father would have them be, for they shall be the hands of the Father made manifest, and they shall touch 'them' and make them whole, even as the blessed Sananda is prepared to touch them and make them whole. And so be it that many shall walk among them as the hands of the Father and they have but to seek them out and they shall find and they shall be blest of them. So be it and Beleis.

<u>I am come that the veil may be torn away! and that ye may know us as we know thee</u>: and that ye may see the light of the Christ and walk therein. So be it and Selah. Blest are they which seek for they shall be greatly blest of them which are sent, so be ye prepared to receive them in the name of the Father, Son and Holy Ghost, Amen and Selah. <u>Be ye at Peace and Poise for ye shall receive more from this source and ye shall know that which ye see and hear is of the Divine Ordinance and that ye are being prepared for greater things! for the "greater part,"</u> and so be it and Beleis. And be ye as one which is of a mind to receive that which is given unto them which are sent out for thee, and so shall it profit thee much. And be ye as one which can comprehend that which is given unto thee, and so be it and Selah.

I am the Worthy Grand Master of the Inner Temple.

## Sananda

Blest of my being: Be ye prepared to receive that which has been kept for 'them' for this time, and so be it given unto them in the name of the Father, Son and Holy Ghost, Amen and Beleis.

Blest ones, which are my sheep, and which I call my own, and which the Father has given unto me. Shall ye not see me and shall ye not walk and talk with me? For I have called thee out from among them. And some of you have heard my voice, and they have made haste unto me, and some have not heard, and they shall be made to hear. For I shall give unto them that which shall cause them to hear. And I shall bring them out from among them.

And ye shall be sibored in the eternal verities. And ye shall be given comprehension. And ye shall be at peace, and ye shall not hunger, nor shall ye know sorrow. For it is given unto me to care for my own and I shall be unto thee all that ye shall have need of. And so be it and Beleis.

I am come into the world of men at the appointed hour, and I have kept my covenant with thee: for I said I should return unto thee - so have I, and I have gone the long way to keep my word: for it is given unto me to keep my word. And as I have promised thee, "I have prepared a place for thee," and now it is the day of thy preparation.

And as ye have been told, it shall be given unto every man to stand before the throne and to receive his sonship. And for the have I come that ye may receive that which is kept for thee. So be it that ye shall be given a new part and ye shall be prepared to receive it in the name of the Father, Son and Holy Ghosts, Amen and Beleis. Be ye as ones which know wherein ye are staid and be ye alert, and watchful, for there are many sent, unto thee that they may bring thee out. And ye shall receive them in the name of Father which has sent them unto thee. For it is the day of much activity, and ye shall not be deceived for we guard "our own" and give unto them comprehension to know them which are sent.

Yet, ye shall pray for comprehension, and ye shall be unto her thy self true, and ye shall have no 'false gods' for ye shall seek thy salvation thru the Father, and ye shall not seek in dark places, for therein is not Light. And ye shall be as one which can see the Light of the Christ, and walk therein. And ye shall not be as the Child of Light.

Ye shall not ask any man's opinion nor council with the dead, for it is not given unto them to deliver thee out of darkness: and forget not that they too seek their freedom. And so be ye as one which can keep thy own council, and be thy own carter, and ye shall find thy way into the place which I have prepared for thee. And so be ye prepared to receive me, for I shall reveal myself unto them which are so prepared to receive me. So be it and Beleis. Blest are they which seek me out, for they shall receive that which I have kept for them.

And now the day of revelation is come ye shall stand in the secret place of my abode and ye shall see and hear, and ye shall know that which ye hear and see. And ye shall council with me and ye shall be made to comprehend that which I shall say unto thee. So be ye prepared and as ye are prepared to receive me ye shall be prepared to receive of the Father which has sent me. And as ye are prepared to receive me so shall ye receive them which I shall send unto thee as my emissaries - for they shall go out before me - even as my Father has sent me out before Him! And so be it that many shall be sent in the name of the Father, Son and Holy Ghost, Amen and Beleis.

I am thy elder brother and servant of the Christ, which ye shall come to know. So, be it and Beleis. Sananda, Order of The Emerald Cross and Brotherhood of the Seven Rays.

Blest of my being: Be ye at Peace and Poise and ye shall receive that which has been prepared for 'them' by the Blessed Mother Sarah, and ye shall give it unto them in the name of the Father, Son and Holy Ghost, amen and Beleis.

## Blessed Mother Sarah

Blessed child, which has gone out from me which I have held so close: Be ye prepared to return unto me, and so be it that ye shall receive thy inheritance in full: And ye shall return unto 'them' as a living witness of thy Fathers mercy and love. And ye shall go out among them and ye shall touch 'them' <u>and they shall become awake!</u> <u>and ye shall be given that which the Father would have thee be</u>. And ye shall give unto 'them' as he shall give unto thee. For ye shall be unto 'them' his hands. So be it and Selah.

I am come that ye may receive that which ye shall give unto them, and it shall serve to prepare them, for it is given unto many to await thy coming. So be it that they shall be prepared to receive thee. And it shall be given unto them to know thee, and they shall receive in the name of the Father, which shall send thee out. So be it and

Selah. Now ye may be as one which has free passport into the place wherein I am, for all barriers shall be removed and ye shall pass freely, and so be it and Beleis. Be ye at peace and poise and ye shall be put into thy new place wherein are many which await to receive thee. And so be it that there shall be great joy and much gladness. And for that have I come unto thee, that ye may be prepared to enter into my place of abode.

And as I have said unto thee before, "I am prepared to be hostess unto thee, and ye shall be glad to be in my place," So be it and Selah. I am given unto hospitality and I shall be prepared to receive all which are prepared to enter wherein I am. <u>So be it that there shall be a great coming together and there shall be great rejoicing through out the kingdom. And so be it that ye shall remember each other and ye shall be as ones long away and which have returned from a long journey</u>.

So be it that ye shall go out into darkness no more, for ye shall know thy source, and ye shall separate thyself no more. Ye shall know that which is meant by the Christ, and ye shall walk in the Light thereof forevermore. And so be it and Beleis and Selah. And ye shall be as one which has returned unto me, and ye shall be as I am, and ye shall be equal unto me. And that is thy lawful inheritance: for are ye not one of mine, and have ye not gone out from me, and do I not give of myself that ye may return unto me? And is it not said that all that I am ye shall become? And so be it and Selah. I am thy Mother Sarah and the Fortune of the Father, and to whom ye shall return, so be it and Selah.

Blest of my being: Ye shall now receive that which is prepared for thee by the one and only Osiris, and that which he has prepared for 'them' - and ye shall give it unto them in the name of the Father, Son and Holy Ghost. So be it and Beleis.

## Osiris

Blest of my being, and of my presence: For it is given unto me, Osiris, of the Temple of Osiris, to welcome thee into the place wherein I abide. And as ye have received that which has been kept for thee ye shall have free passport into the place wherein I am. and ye shall go and come at will and ye shall not be limited by any law of earth: <u>for ye shall be free from the gravitation of the earth and free from the attraction of the moon. And ye shall go and come as ye will</u>. And ye shall be as one of us. And as the Father has given unto me that which is my inheritance I know that which is given unto thee, for it is not given unto the uninitiated to know the joy and thankfulness which is given unto the one which has received his freedom.

And so be it that there are many which shall await thy coming, and so be it that their waiting shall end. So be it and Selah.

Be ye at peace and poise and one shall come unto thee and he shall bring thee into the secret place wherein ye shall receive that which is prepared for thee and for that have ye waited. So be it that ye shall receive him into thy place in the name of the Father, Son and Holy Ghost. So be it and Selah. Be ye as one so liberated; and so be it that ye shall stand before the throne of the Father, and before the twenty-four elders. And they shall give unto thee that which they have kept for thee: for each has kept a part for thee and ye shall receive it in the name of the most High Living God, and ye shall know that which is meant by the Christ, and ye shall see the "Light" and ye shall walk therein forevermore. So be it and Selah.

One which has gone out from the place wherein I am shall come unto thee and he shall be unto thee thy hands and thy feet, and he shall bring thee into the place wherein I am, and ye shall receive that which I have kept for thee. And so be it that there shall be great joy and much gladness. And ye shall be given thy new name, and thy shield which shall be unto thee all things.

Ye shall be given that which shall serve as thy passport into all the secret places of the earth. And ye shall be given a place within them wherein ye may call home: and wherein ye may have thy place of abode. So be it and Selah.

Be ye at peace and poise and ye shall receive of my love and wisdom, and I shall be as thy hands and thy feet, and I shall stand ready to serve thee in the name of the Most High. So be it and Selah. I am thy older brother, and thy servant. And wherein have I said: "I am prepared to receive them which are prepared." So be it. I am Osiris, of The Temple of Osiris. Recorded by Sister Thedra.

# Part #40

Blest of my being: Be ye at peace and poise - and ye shall receive of the one and only Brother Zamu - and that which he has for thee - and it shall be sent unto them that they may know that which is in store for them which so prepares themself to receive of the Father's Love and Grace and Mercy -- So be it given unto thee in the Name of the Father - Son and Holy Ghost -- Amen and Beleis ---

## Zamu

Blest of my being: Be ye blest of us which await thy coming - for long have we awaited this day -- And so be it that there shall be many brot in from thy place ---

And so be it that they may be prepared to receive their freedom -- And for that have we the Sibors of the Losolo been sent that they may be prepared -- And as they are prepared so shall they receive -- And now that it is come that ye shall be brot into this place there shall be much rejoicing! for it has been given unto us to await thy coming -- And now there shall be many to receive thee -- And be ye as one which has received that which has been given unto thee as thy inheritance - for the Father has willed it that ye may pass the great barrier -- And ye shall return unto them as the emissary of the Temple of Osiris - and we thy Sibors -- And so be it that they shall be given that which ye shall be given for them - and they shall profit thereby - and so be it and Selah ---

Now it is cause for much rejoicing - and there shall be much music - and many shall sing unto the Father praise for the fulfillment of the covenant which they have made with Him -- And long have they waited - for in the beginning of thy sojourn within the Earth they gave unto the Father their solemn oath that they should watch thee - and that ye should be kept for this day -- And so shall ye return victorious -- So be it and Selah ---

Blest are they which have kept thee and guarded thee - and now they shall receive their reward - and so be it and Selah -- And give unto them praise and thanks for their loyalty and their love - and ye shall receive of them their part which they have kept for thee -- So be it and Selah ---

I am one which has awaited thy coming - so be it my joy shall know no bounds -- So be it that I shall receive them in joy and thanksgiving ---

I am thy servant and Brother Zamu - of the Temple of Osiris--

Blest of my being: Be ye at peace and poise and be ye prepared to receive that which shall be given unto thee by the blessed Brother of Light Maroni - for he has prepared a part for thee - which shall be sent unto them -- And they shall have that which is given unto them of and by him -- So be it and Beleis ---

**Maroni**

Blest of my being: Be ye blest of my presence - for I come that ye may receive of my love and wisdom -- And be ye at peace and poise - for one shall come unto thee and he shall bring thee into the secret place of my abode and ye shall be as a guest in my house -- And I shall give unto thee that which I have kept for thee - for it shall be my joy to receive thee -- And it has been given unto me to be one

86

which has awaited thy coming - and there shall be great joy and much gladness -- And so be it that there shall be many to receive thee - for when one is brot in there is great rejoicing thruout the Kingdom ---

And there shall be signs and manifestations of thy coming - and they which are alert may see and know that one has returned home -- And so be it that many shall come out of the Earth - and they shall be prepared for that -- And as they are prepared so shall they be brot in and they shall not wait for them which have not prepared themself -- So be it that they shall be given as they are prepared to receive -- -

And so be it that they which have presented themself for preparation shall be groomed and prepared -- And they shall be given that which is prepared for them -- And be ye as one which has received thy new part - and ye shall be given that which I have kept for thee -- And so be it and Selah ---

I am given unto patience - and long have I waited for thy return -- For at the time of thy going out ye said unto me: "I shall return - and I shall remember that which I have said unto thee" -- And so shall ye - and ye shall be as one which has returned unto me victorious -- For it is given unto me to be one of thy fathers - within one of thy embodiments within the Earth - and ye have not remembered that part of thy sojourn -- And so be it that ye shall recall all that ye have forgotten - and it shall be part of thy inheritance to remember -- So be it and Selah. ---

Some shall be given to remember that which they have said within their sleep -- And some shall hear that which is recorded upon the "eth" and they shall be bewildered - and yet they shall not be afraid -- For it shall be given unto them to understand that which is about them - and that which they shall come to know as natural law -- And they shall seek comprehension of the law which shall be revealed unto them ---

So be it that we shall come unto them and sibor them in the law of Losoloes - and they shall be given as they can consume -- So be it and Selah -- Be ye blest of them within the place of my abode - and give unto the Father praise for thy deliverance -- And so shall ye be blest of Him -- And so be it and Beleis ---

I am thy servant in the Light of the Christ - and thy Brother Maroni - of the Emerald Cross and the Brotherhood of the 7 Rays--

Blest of my being: Be ye prepared to receive that which is prepared for thee by the blessed Sister of Light Saboni - for She has prepared a part for them - and ye shall give it unto them in the Name of the Father - Son and Holy Ghost -- So be it and Beleis---

## Sister Saboni

Blest of my being: Be ye as one which has received thy inheritance - and be ye as one which has upon thy head a crown -- And ye shall come into the place wherein I am and ye shall be blest of the Father -- For He has remembered thee - and He has been prepared for the day of thy return - and now there shall be great joy and gladness that one has returned ---

So be ye blest of us - which have gone the Royal Road -- And be ye prepared to enter into my place of abode - for ye shall receive

88

within my place instructions for thy new part - and ye shall go into my home land prepared for thy part -- And ye shall be received in honor and in part -- Ye shall not falter - nor shall ye want - for many are waiting for thy coming - they are prepared to receive thee -- <u>And ye shall go into the land of Spain - and therein ye shall be received by them which are alert - and which have been warned that "One shall come from out of the Inner Temple"</u> ---

And so shall ye go into the secret places wherein there are records which have been kept for this day and ye shall read - and ye shall be given that which ye shall give unto them - and they shall know that which has been given unto them by thee is from the secret place of the blessed Brother Sananda (Jesus of Nazareth) - for one has given them that much: that <u>"One should come bearing proof"</u>-- <u>And they shall give unto thee credit</u> - and they shall give praise for the "new revelation" ---

And so be it that ye shall find thy own people which are within that place - and ye shall give unto them that which is for them -- And so be it that they shall receive thee in joy and gladness -- And so be it Selah -- Be ye as one which has prepared thyself to receive thy inheritance - for it is said that <u>"Ye become that for which ye are prepared"</u> - and so be it -- And as ye have been called out from among them ye have answered - and so be it ye shall be brot into the Inner Temple and ye shall partake of that which is kept for thee -- And so be it in the Name of the Most High - and Selah ---

Be ye at peace and poise and ye shall receive of the Father - Son and Holy Ghost - Amen and Selah -- Since ye have been called out from among them ye have received many of us from the Inner Temple -- Now we wait to receive thee - and there shall be great joy and much gladness - for it is a day of fulfillment -- And ye shall be given that for which ye have waited -- And I have a part for thee - and ye shall receive it in love and mercy - and ye shall carry it with dignity and gladness -- And so be ye prepared for thy enua -- And ye shall with surety - and ye shall be glad for thy deliverance -- And blest are they which have received of their heritage -- And blest are they which come into the place wherein I am - for they shall return into darkness no more -- And so be it and Beleis ---

Blest shall ye be for there are many which wait to receive thee - and so shall there be a great coming together - and much praise - for there shall be music - and songs of praise - for as one is brot in it is cause for great rejoicing -- So be it and Beleis and Selah ---

I am thy Sister Saboni - of the Order of the Emerald Cross - and of the Inner Temple of Osiris --

Blest of my being: Be ye prepared to receive that which is prepared for thee by the blessed Brother of Light Osiris -- And ye shall receive it for them in the Name of the Father - Son and Holy Ghost -- Amen and Beleis ---

# Part #41

## Osiris

Beloved ones of Earth: Wherein is it said: "Man - Know thyself" -- And this is the first law -- And it is given unto each to come to know that which they are -- And for that has the new dispensation been given - that all men may know that which they are and that which is their inheritance -- And long has the child of Earth wandered in darkness -- Now it is come that many are sent out from the realms of Light to bring him in - into his rightful place and to give him deliverance from bondage -- And it is given unto me to have a part with thee - and a part which shall be unto thee profitable -- For long have I sibored the child of Earth - and many have I instructed in the laws of the Losoloe -- And within the time which is near ye shall be called - and ye shall be wise to heed the call - and ye shall be brot into the place wherein I am - and ye shall be instructed in the Temple of Osiris - and ye shall be as one come alive ---

For ye have been in the places of darkness so long ye are as the "living dead" -- And ye have forgotten thy identity -- Ye have moved as one drunken -- And ye have gone into the temples of idolatry - and ye have not known the Christ! For there has been a great mist before thee - and ye have not seen the Light -- Now it is come that the mist shall be rolled away! - and ye shall see and ye shall walk therein -- And so be it and Selah ---

For the first time I say to thee that thy temples of idolatry shall fall as the temple of Babel! And ye shall stand shorn of all thy gained glory - and of all the opinions - and of all thy purchases -- And ye shall have nothing which to call thy own -- And ye shall call unto the Father - as ye have never before! ---

Be ye prepared for that day! - for it is nigh upon thee - and it shall stand thee four square to be prepared -- Now I say unto thee as so many have said before me: "Be ye prepared" - for within the time which is near ye shall be discomforted - and ye shall have no place wherein to lay thy head ---

And ye shall call out - and ye may be late! - and sad are they which are late - for it is said: "Blest are they which seek the Light early" -- And so be it and Selah --

And be ye as one which can comprehend that which I say unto thee - for it is said simply - and in few words - and it is given that every one may comprehend -- And ye shall have no possible excuse for not being prepared! For many shall go out into all the Earth - and the cry shall be sounded from every place - and they shall be as sentinels within the place wherein they shall be sent -- For ye shall not be allowed forget - for we are diligent and true to our trust -- And so be it and Beleis ----

So be ye true unto thyself - and give unto them within thy care that which is given unto thee -- Ye shall prepare them even as we thy Sibors endeavor to prepare thee -- And blest are they which are prepared to receive of that which we have for them -- And so be it that a voice shall ring out thru the land and ye shall answer - and make straitway unto it! And ye shall be as one delivered up -- And so shall ye be glad for thy knowing -- And so be it that many await to deliver thee up -- And so be it in the Name of the Most High -- And so be it and Selah -- I am thy Older Brother of the Temple of

92

Osiris - and of the Emerald Cross - and of the Brotherhood of the Seven Rays - Osiris -- Recorded by Sister Thedra --

Blest of my being: Be ye prepared to receive that which is prepared for them by the blessed Sister Nada -- And it shall be given unto them in the Name of the Father - Son and Holy Ghost -- Amen and Beleis ---

## Sister Nada

Beloved Sister of the Emerald Cross - and which shall be my hands: Ye shall be blest of them within the Inner Temple - and ye shall be as one of us -- And ye shall know us as we know thee - and so be it and Selah -- It is a glorious new day when we shall walk hand in hand and when the mist shall roll away - and ye shall know us as we know thee! And so be it cause for much rejoicing - and so be it and Selah -- Be ye one which has received thy sonship - and be ye at peace and poise - and ye shall receive of the Father - Son and Holy Ghost -- And so be it and Selah -- And be it so that many await thy coming - and now that ye have received of me in the Name of the Father - Son and Holy Ghost - so shall I receive thee in His Grace and Mercy -- And ye shall be as one come alive - and ye shall not return into darkness - never more!

And so be it that there shall be many brot in in the time which is near -- For as it is given unto us to have the greater vision - and we see and know that which is and that which shall be -- So shall they receive thee in love and joy within the place wherein ye shall be sent -- And ye shall lift them up for as the Father has sent thee unto them so shall ye be received in His name -- And they shall be as ones

93

made to comprehend that which ye shall be given for them - and ye shall be received in honor and dignity -- So be it and Beleis ---

Blest shall they be which do receive them which are sent out from the Inner Temple - for they shall receive of the Father - Son and Holy Ghost -- So be it and Beleis -- Before thee is a plan which has been prepared within the Inner Temple by the Most Worthy Grand Master - and He has given it unto us - thy Sibors to fulfill -- And it shall be revealed unto them which are so prepared to receive - and ye shall be given as ye are prepared -- And forget not this is the day of preparation -- And ye shall be brot to account for thy drunkenness and for thy idolatry - so be up and about thy preparation - and ye shall be given that which shall sober thee and that were which shall profit thee ---

And now it is given unto me to be one of thy Sibors - and I shall come unto thee and sibor thee in ways which ye do not comprehend at present -- Yet ye shall grow in strength and wisdom --

And ye shall be as a spark fanned into a great flame! - and ye shall come to know thy oneness with thy Source - and ye shall come to know that which is thy inheritance -- And ye shall be brot into the place wherein I am - where ye shall receive unto thyself that which has been kept for thee -- And so be it that ye shall be free from thy bondage and that which has bound thee -- And so be it as ye will it -- And so be it and Selah ---

I am thy Sister in the secret place of the Most High - and of the Order of the Emerald Cross and of the Temple of Osiris -- Blest are they which come into these places -- And so be it and Selah ---

I am thy Sister Nada –

Blest of my being: Ye shall now be prepared to receive of the one and only Beautealu and that which he has prepared for them -- And so be it given unto them in the Name of the Most High -- And so be it and Beleis ---

## Beautealu

Blest of my being and of my presence: Be ye as my hands made manifest unto them that they may receive that which I have for them - and that which I have received of the Father -- And so be it that they shall be given comprehension to know that which I have said unto them -- For there shall be many which shall bear witness of me and many shall be sent that they may know that which I say unto them is valid - and it shall be given unto them to have signs manifested unto them -- And they shall have their "miracles" - and so be it that they shall know us -- And they shall be unto themself true and they shall hear us out ---

For it shall be given unto them in part - and they which stand still and listen shall be wiser -- And they shall be rewarded - for it is given in such a manner for a purpose - and therein is wisdom -- And be ye of a mind to hear me out for I am of a mind to finish that which I begin -- And it is given unto me to prepare thee for thy new place and thy new part -- And ye have had many say unto thee that "The day of preparation is here"-- And so it is! And so be it that ye shall not be given time to forget! - for there shall be much activity and ye shall read as ye run - for no place shall ye find to rest - for it is come that "all hands shall be on deck and prepared" ---

95

For at any moment ye may be called out and ye shall be wise to be prepared - for it is said that the time of great change is at hand -- And so it is -- And so shall there be great changes which shall change the surface of the Earth - And not any man can say the exact moment - and yet we know the time is nigh -- And be ye prepared - for great is the girth of the Earth - and within She is seething - She is heavy within - and She is anxious to be delivered and She shall be glad to be delivered!

And many are working that ye may be delivered before she is -- And ye shall be removed before She shall be given in labor -- And so be it that many stand ready to receive thee upon the horizon of the Earth -- And ye shall give unto them credit for being prepared to receive thee -- For long have they been prepared for the day of chaos -- And ye have given no thot of them which have prepared themself that ye may be delivered up -- And be ye fruitful and give unto the Father credit for thy being - and give unto thy guardians credit for thy well-being -- And so shall it profit thee -- And so be it and Beleis -- Blest are they which give thanks for their well-being - for the Father shall hear thee and He is not deceived by hollow words -- He knows what is in thy heart and it is given unto Him to see and know that which ye are -- And it is said that there are none so foolish as to try to deceive the Father - for it is given unto Him to see into thy heart and to reward thee in like manner -- For He has given unto thee free will - and as ye portion out into Him ye have portioned out unto thyself -- And so be it and Beleis -- So be ye as wise as a serpent and silent as the sphinx - and give unto thyself that which shall profit thee -- For it is given unto thee to be forewarned - and to be so warned is to be prepared -- And so be it that ye shall be given as ye can comprehend - in the Name of the Father - Son and Holy Ghost have I come unto thee -- So be it and Selah -- I am thy older Brother Beautealu - Son of the Posied - and of the School of the 7 Rays --

Blest of my being: Ye shall now receive of the one and only Brother Bor - and that which he has for them -- And it shall be given unto them in the Name of the Father - Son and Holy Ghost-- Amen and Beleis ----

## Brother Bor

Blest of my being: Be ye blest of my presence - for I am come unto thee out of the Inner Temple - and I have given unto thee of myself that ye may come to know the Christ - and that ye may receive that which the Father has willed unto thee - and ye shall be given comprehension to know that which I say unto thee ---

For it is now come that many are coming into the Earth out of the Inner Temple - and they are giving of themself in love and mercy that ye may know "The smallness of thy tiny red star" - and ye shall be made to know how small! For it is given unto us thy Brothers of the higher realms - to know whereof we speak when we say unto thee that thy Earth shall have a new berth -- For it is given unto us to know - for we have prepared Her for Her new part and for Her new berth -- And She shall slip out of Her present berth into the new -- And we have worked that there shall be as little, panic and chaos as possible - And it is with thy love and thy cooperation that this shall be accomplished -- For within the time which is allotted unto us - we shall come unto thee and sibor thee - and ye shall be aware of us and of our presence -- And ye shall give us credence and port ---

97

And we shall cause them to comprehend that which we give unto thee -- For it is the better part of wisdom to be prepared -- For can ye not see the fortune of them which are unprepared? And can ye not see the wisdom of thy preparation? For now it is come that the Earth has many labor pains - and who can say the hour? And for that do we wait -- And so be it that there are many which stand guard - and at the helm for the purpose of rescuing thee -- And there shall be many unprepared and yet many shall be prepared ---

And sad is the one which is unprepared - for I know! I have seen the hollowness of their eyes -- I have heard the moans and the cries - and I have given unto them succor which is a poor poultice - for therein is the folly of waiting -- And so be it that ye shall be forewarned and fore prepared - for it shall be given unto thee as ye will it -- And so be it that ye may be unto thyself true and seek thy salvation within the Father - and give unto Him the praise and the glory for thy being -- And give unto thy Guardians thanks for thy well-being ---

And be ye blest of the Father - Son and Holy Ghost -- I am thy Brother Bor - of the Inner Temple - and so be ye prepared to enter therein -- Amen and Selah -- Recorded by Sister Thedra --

# Part #42

Bless of my being: Ye shall now receive that which is prepared for thee by the one and only Esmeraldo - and ye shall give it unto them which are prepared to receive of him - and that which he has for them -- So be it given unto them in His Name - Amen and Beleis --

## Esmeraldo

Blessed ones which are prepared to receive of my words - and that which I am prepared to give unto thee: Be ye blest and be ye prepared to receive that which I am prepared to give unto thee -- For it is my part to give unto thee "comfort" in the time of stress and discomfort -- And as ye are prepared for thy new part which shall be given unto thee - ye may be one which has not prepared thyself to be delivered up -- So it is given unto me - "The Comforter" to stand ready to administer unto thee -- And so be it that there shall be many - yet I am the one to whom they shall be responsible ---

And be it 'the poor part of wisdom to wait for the comforter! When ye may be delivered out of discomfort wherein ye shall know no suffering and sorrow -- And yet there shall be many which are unprepared and they shall be caught up short of their course -- And they shall be glad to receive me and my partners which are sent unto thee of the Father - in His great compassion and mercy ---

And so be it that ye shall be mindful of us which stand in wait and thy service -- For many a call do we answer unaware unto thee - and ye shall become aware of that which goes on around thee - and ye shall profit thereby -- And be ye as one which can comprehend that which is said unto thee -- And be ye prepared that ye may not have to call unto us -- For it shall serve thee well to be prepared to enter into the place which is prepared for thee in full consciousness and in full recognition of thy sponsors and of thy help -- And to know from whence it cometh! And them which are not so prepared shall go in deep sleep - and they shall have their memory blanked from them - that they may not remember their loved ones - that they may not have the burden of sorrow which would be unto them a "millstone" -- So be ye wise and give unto thyself which shall be unto thee thy deliverance from suffering and sorrow -- So be ye blest of us and of our presence - and be ye as wise as a serpent and silent as a sphinx - and prepare thyself to receive the Greater Part" - and so shall it profit thee ---

I am at thy service in the Name of the Most High -- I am thy Brother - and thy Sibor Esmeraldo - of the Order of the Emerald Cross and the Brotherhood of the 7 Rays---

Blest of my being: Ye shall now receive that which is prepared for thee by the one and only Orpheus - and it shall be given unto them which are prepared to receive it -- And they shall receive it in the Name of the Father - Son and Holy Ghost -- So be it and Beleis ---

## Orpheus

Bless of my being: Be ye prepared to receive that which is given unto me of the Father - that ye may receive Him thru me -- And so be it that I shall give unto thee as ye are prepared to receive -- And so be it that ye may have a greater capacity for learning ---

And for that have we come unto thee from out of the realms of light that ye may be brot out of darkness - and that ye may come into thy rightful estate -- And that ye may know the Christ -- And so be ye prepared for that which shall be revealed unto thee -- And as ye are prepared so shall he receive -- I am come unto thee from out of the silence - for it has not been given unto me to speak for a while unto the child of Earth ---

In time past they walked with me and they knew me well! And there came a day of much darkness when it was not permissible for us to enter into thy world of darkness -- And we had but to wait for the new dawn and the new dispensation when ye would receive us in love and harmony ---

And now that the door is open unto us we shall come in again and we shall commune free -- And we shall give unto thee much which has been kept for this day. And ye shall receive as ye are prepared to receive - and so be it and Selah -- I am come that ye may receive my part which has been held in trust for thee until this time - and so be it that it shall profit thee ---

And now that it is come that ye shall pass the great barrier many shall be brot into the temples wherein ye may partake of our love – our art and music – our science and our beauty – which is beyond that which ye know -- Ye shall stand speechless and in awe! And ye shall know into what depths of darkness ye have descended! And ye shall be prepared for the new age - and ye shall be given that which ye have prepared thyself for -- And that which shall bring into the new day the science and art and music and the beauty for which we have worked for eons -- And it shall be given unto thee to be part of the glorious New Age! And So be ye prepared to enter into the

Temple wherein I abide - and ye shall be given passport unto this place which is the part which has been closed unto thee for so long -- And so be it that I shall be glad to receive thee - and ye shall be glad for thy preparation -- And so be it and Selah---

I am thy Older Brother and thy servant in the Name of the Most High -- I await thee - and be ye at peace and posie - and ye shall be received in love and understanding -- Thy Sibor Orpheus of the Brotherhood of the Emerald Cross ---

Blest of my being: Be ye prepared to receive that which is prepared for thee by the one and only Osiris - and that which he has prepared for them -- And so shall it be given unto them in the name of the Father - Son and Holy Ghost -- So be it and Beleis ---

**Osiris**

Be ye blest of my being - and be ye blest of my presence -- I am come unto thee that ye may give unto them which are ready to receive that which I shall be prepared to give unto them -- And that they may know that which I am prepared to reveal unto them -- And for that have I waited - that they may receive me -- And that whey may be brot into the place wherein I am -- And so be it and Beleis-- I am given unto patience and I shall wait! And is it not said that I many shall be brot out of the Earth into this place - and so be it -- And it shall be fortuned unto them to return unto the Earth as My emissaries - and they shall be the ones which shall be the "lamps in the windows" - for it shall be given unto them to prepare them which are prepared to receive -- For it is come that the children of Earth are not sufficient unto the new age -- And they shall need much help from the higher realms ---

102

And as it is given unto the adolescent to need the help and wisdom of the parents - so shall the Earth need that which She shall receive of us -- And as the adolescent She shall feel Herself sufficient until the day of disaster - then She shall cry aloud for help - and She shall be a bit late -- Yet We shall be unto Her balm----

Now it is said that in these days – "There are great scientists and great musicians - great artists - and wherein are we lacking?" And I say unto thee that ye are lacking in all thy departments For ye have perfected nothing! As ye reach out into the unknown ye are as foolish children with new toys! For ye have given much credit unto thyself and wherein have ye profited by thy toys and thy so called science? For the day shall come when thy toys shall no longer obey thy will -- And ye shall be stript of all thy glory! for ye have not built thy house upon the rock -- And it shall be swept before the wind - and ye shall stand as one speechless and helpless -- For thy plants shall wither for the want of light - thy rivers shall overflow their banks - thy lakes shall have no bounds - and the water shall cover thy roofs - and the fires shall sweep thy forests - and the planes shall fall upon the mountain sides - and the grass shall dry and blow away as chaff -- And ye shall stand helpless!

And ye shall give no credit unto thyself for bringing about such conditions - for therein is no glory! - and yet ye shall say: "look what we have accomplished when ye give unto them the virus which shall torment them - and which shall be unto them 'legirons' " ---

And now I say unto thee as has been said so many times - that ye shall prepare thyself for the day of reckoning is come -- And ye shall seek within the realms of light for thy deliverance from bondage - for ye shall not find it within the realm of darkness -- And again I say unto thee that ye shall seek thy salvation within the Father – and ye shall be brot out of darkness -- And ye shall not subject thy brother into the tests which ye call "scientific"-- And ye shall not be spared the consequence of thy experiments with the atom! And ye shall not give thy brother that which shall be unto him torment! For ye have not seen that which shall result of such experiments - for it carries into the third and fourth embodiment -- And they are crying within the dark places of the astral world for deliverance - and they remember that which has been said and done while ye have thot them asleep -- They are not asleep when they are under anesthetic - and they are given to know what is going on within their realm - and they have said that which should profit thee to remember - And ye men of medicine shall heed what I say unto thee - for ye are but children which have not yet reached the age of accountability -- And ye shall be given that which ye can comprehend ---

Ye shall not be accountable unto them which ye have purchased but ye shall be accountable unto the Father - for He has not willed it that ye so torment thy brothers - and ye shall be called to account for that which ye have done in the name of "science and progress"-- Now that the new day is come ye shall turn from thy old ways and ye shall seek that which shall be given unto thee of the Father -- Ye which so prepare thyself shall be brot into the temple of healing - wherein ye may learn the laws which govern all things - Ye shall have thy hands made in the likeness of the Father's -- Ye shall "touch" the infirmed and the sick and they shall be made new and whole -- And ye shall be given to know that which has caused the sickness - and to heal the cause - to remove the cause -- So be it and Selah -- And I have given unto thee that which is given unto me of the Father - so shall it profit thee -- And so be it and Selah -- I am thy Brother of the Temple of Osiris and of the Brotherhood of the Emerald Cross -- Osiris ---

Bless of my being: Ye shall now receive of the one and only Archangel Gabriel - and that which he has prepared for them -- And it shall be given unto them which are prepared to receive of him and that which he has for them -- And be it given unto them in the Name of the Father - Son and Holy Ghost -- So be it and Beleis---

**Archangel Gabriel**

Blessed Sister of the Emerald Cross: Be ye blest of my being and of my presence -- And be ye as my hands manifest unto them - and ye shall be blest of the Father - Son and Holy Ghost -- So be it and Beleis -- I am come unto thee that they which are prepared may receive that which I am prepared to give unto them -- So be it that they shall profit therefrom -- And ye shall give unto them that which shall be given into them for them - for ye shall be brot into the star ship - and ye shall be given instructions which shall serve thee well --

For in the days ahead ye shall go out into the "world of men" and ye shall give unto them that which ye have been given upon the star ship - and ye shall be unto then the hands of the Father made manifest - for they shall know that which is given unto them for the new day -- And they shall be prepared to receive thee as the emissary of the Archangel Gabriel of the Star Ship -- And they shall be given as they are prepared to receive -- And none which are not able to comprehend shall be given - none which have not prepared themself shall be given -- And them which are so prepared shall be given that which they are able to comprehend -- So be it and Selah ---

I am prepared to receive them which shall be prepared -- For in the time which is near I shall draw the star ship near unto the Earth and I shall receive thereupon them which are being prepared -- And they shall return as my emissaries -- For the time is come when ye shall have free communication with them of the higher realms and ye which are so prepared shall go and come at will and in wisdom - - And ye shall know us - thy guardians - and ye shall be glad for thy knowing -- And ye shall be glad for thy new part - and for thy new place -- And so shall it profit thee ---

And many have gathered in council for thy preparation - for it is indeed sad that ye are so deaf -- And that ye are so dead that ye have not stirred! For we have given unto thee much which should awaken thee -- And so be it that some shall be sent out from my place and they shall be as the mouth and the hands of the Father - for they shall say that which He would have them say unto thee -- And they shall go into all the places of the Earth -- And they shall give into them to give unto the ones so prepared to receive -- And they shall not say they have not known! For it shall be offered unto everyone which has <u>a pore (body)</u> to understand that which is said unto them -- <u>For simplicity shall be the keynote and prepare thyself shall be the cry!</u> ---

And ye shall be prepared for that which ye shall receive - and as ye are prepared so shall ye receive - for ye shall be given according to thy preparation -- And so shall ye be given as ye can comprehend -- Many shall be given new bodies and they shall be made new - and they shall not taste of death ---

For it is given unto man to overcome death - and he shall step into his new body made whole -- And this is the plan which the blessed Sananda gave unto man so long ago - yet they have not accepted that which the Father has willed him -- And so be it that the day is come when many shall receive their inheritance in full -- So be it and Beleis ---

I am thy Guardian and Sibor and thy Brother - of the Order of the Emerald Cross - and of the Brotherhood of the Seven Rays --- Gabriel of the Star Ship ---

Recorded by Sister Thedra of the Emerald Cross - and of the School of the Seven Rays ---

# Part #43

Blest of my being: Be ye prepared to receive that which is prepared for thee by the one and only Polaris - for he has prepared a part for them - and it shall be given unto them in the Name of the Father - Son and Holy Ghost -- So be it and Beleis ---

## Polaris

Beloved child of Earth: Be ye blest of my being - and of my presence -- For I am come unto thee that ye may know me - and that ye may give unto them which do not know me -- For it is now come that many shall become aware of their benefactors -- For it is we which are responsible for their well-being -- And is not time that they know us? For the new age is come when they shall be as ones awakened unto us - and unto our parts -- For in the time which is near they shall be reminded of us ---

And now ye shall give unto them this part - and this shall be my first part for them -- And as they shall grow in comprehension shall I give unto them -- At the time the Earth was formed and sent out on Her appointed course - She was given them which should be responsible for Her welfare - for Her balance - for Her poise - for Her weight and girth - and for Her grooming for the Earthly habitation -- And it was given unto me to have the part for balancing Her - and to keep Her in Her appointed course - and to give unto Her berth - And now it is come that She shall be moved into another berth - and She is being groomed for that - and She shall be slipt out of Her present berth as gently as possible and with as little chaos as possible ---

108

And there shall be a part which ye of the Earth shall have with this going out - and ye shall be prepared if ye but will it so -- For as we the ones which are preparing the Earth are preparing Her - so are thy Sibors preparing thee -- And they know whereof they speak when they say there shall be chaos and panic! <u>For they are given i to panic! And they are not given to peace and poise</u> -- And for that are we the Sibors of the Losolo working without ceasing that they may be at peace and poise - for in this manner shall we move the Earth into Her new berth with little discomfort to Her and none unto thee -- <u>For it is so planned that everyone shall be moved from the surface of the Earth - and that they shall be moved into the place which is prepared for them</u> - in ease and with the precision of a well drilled army - for they which are to put thee into thy new place have been "drilled" -- They have been prepared for this day of evacuation - and so be ye prepared to receive them - for they come unto thee as thy benefactors - and they shall deliver thee up - and they shall be unto thee thy hands and thy feet---

And many are sent unto thee to prepare thee - for it is the better part of wisdom to be prepared -- And for the first time I say unto thee that there are many which sit in council for thy benefit that ye may be prepared ---

If ye could but look in on the Sibors wherein they are in council and see and hear the plans for thy deliverance - ye would be up and about thy own preparation -- For it is the greatest plan which has been inaugurated within the history of man -- For it has been said that everyone shall receive his inheritance which is given unto him of the Father -- And ye have no concept of that which He has held in trust for thee! For it is now come when everyone shall be offered his inheritance -- So be it that it shall profit him to accept it -- <u>And ye shall be prepared to sit in council with thy Sibors if ye so will it -- For man is now coming to the age of accountability - when he shall know that which is his inheritance</u> -- And so be It and Selah –

And for this have we waited that we may open our secret chambers unto thee -- And so be it that ye may be prepared to enter -- I am one which shall welcome thee - and I shall sibor thee in the laws of the Losolo when ye are so prepared to receive -- And so be it and Beleis -- I am thy Older Brother and Benefactor and Sibor Polaris - of the Inner Temple ---

Blest of my being: Be ye prepared to receive that which is prepared for them by our beloved Brother Zamu -- For he has prepared it in the Name of the Father - Son and Holy Ghost -- So be it and Beleis ---

**Zamu**

Be ye blest of my being -- Be ye as my hands unto them that they may receive that which I have prepared for them ---

I am in the secret place of my abode wherein I am prepared to receive thee - and wherein ye shall be brot - and ye shall be given that which ye shall give unto them -- For it is now come that ye shall come into my place of abode to receive thy instructions for thy new part which ye are to take or to give unto them -- And they shall come to know that "Ye are not being counseled of the dead" -- And be ye as one which knows thy Sibors - and for that have we waited that ye may be prepared to enter into our chambers wherein ye may sit in council with us - and wherein ye may partake of our learning and wisdom which shall be given unto thee as thy heritage - and for this have ye been prepared -- And so be it and Selah ---

Blest are they which are so prepared - for they shall be greatly rewarded -- And ye shall be as of the Father unto them which are not yet prepared to enter into the secret place -- For ye shall be prepared to go unto them with the plan which shall be revealed unto thee in its entirety -- And ye shall give unto them as they are able to comprehend -- So be it and Selah---

And they too shall be brot in as they are prepared -- And such is the plan which is given unto us for its fulfillment -- And ye shall be the recipient of the richness of such a plan -- And for that do we give of ourself - that ye may receive of the Father's Mercy and Love -- And so be it and Selah ---

Will ye not give unto us of thy time and energy that ye may be given that which shall profit thee? And so be it the better part of wisdom! And so be it and Selah -- We which sibor thee know no rest nor sleep - for we are diligent - and we keep constant watch that ye shall not be discomforted --- For it is told them that "There are great forces of darkness built up within the atmosphere of the Earth which await to consume thee" - which shall manifest as pestilence - storms - and the like -- And ye are as the ones which can transmute these forces -- And by thy peace and poise - thy love for all things shall ye transmute them and turn them into the blessed energy which shall be unto thee thy deliverance -- And be ye as wise as a serpent (initiate) and silent as the sphinx -- And say not that ye are the chemist - but keep thy own council and say not that which is of darkness and which is of light -- Forget not that silence is thy fortress and thy shield and buckler - and ye shall grow in strength and

111

wisdom -- So be it and Beleis - and Selah -- I am thy Brother and Sibor Zamu - of the Order of the Emerald Cross –

Blest of my being: Be ye prepared to receive that which is prepared for them by our blessed Sister of Light Saboni -- And it shall be given unto them in the Name of the Father - Son and Holy Ghost -- So be it and Beleis ---

**Sister Saboni**

Blessed Sister of the Emerald Cross: Be ye blest of my presence and that which ye shall receive of me -- Be ye as my hand unto them which are prepared to receive of me - for it shall be given unto thee to come into my place of abode and ye shall counsel with me - and ye shall receive thy instructions for thy part which shall take thee into the land to the east -- And ye shall be given that which shall serve as thy passport into all the places wherein ye shall go ---

And ye shall not want nor shall ye weary -- For it shall be given unto thee to be made new -- And so be it and Selah -- And ye shall be as one which has received thy inheritance ---

And ye shall be one which has prepared thyself for it -- And so shall ye be brot into the secret place wherein ye shall be prepared for the Inner Temple -- And ye shall be as the hands of the Father-Mother made manifest unto them -- Ye shall give unto them as ye receive for them -- And so be it and Selah ---

Be ye prepared to give unto them that which ye shall receive for them - and so be it in the Name of the most High Living God -- Blest are they which receive their inheritance - for they shall know the

Father which has sent them out -- And so be it and Selah -- <u>Be ye at Peace and Poise - and ye shall receive of the Father - Son and Holy Ghost</u> -- So be it and Selah---

Be ye prepared that ye may go into the secret places of the Earth and receive instructions in thy new part - for it shall be given unto thee to be brot out of the Earth - and to have initiations within the Temple of Osiris - and within the secret place of the Most High -- And ye shall return unto the Earth and ye shall give unto them as they are prepared to receive -- So be it and Beleis ---

And for this have ye waited that ye may be prepared -- And now it is come that ye shall be called into the secret place which shall be revealed unto thee - and ye shall be groomed for thy new part which shall take thee into the Temple of Osiris and into the place of the Most High -- And so be it and Beleis -- Blest are the ones which are brot into the secret place for they shall see God the Father -- And they shall be given that which has been kept for them -- So be it and Beleis ---

Be ye as one which has received, thy inheritance in full - and so shall ye receive of Him - and ye shall receive of the Son and Holy Ghost -- And so be it and Beleis -- I am thy Sister Saboni - of the Inner Temple and of the Order of the Emerald Cross ---

Beloved of my being: Be ye prepared to receive that which the blessed Sister of Light Nada - has for them - and it shall be given unto them in the Name of the Father - Son and Holy Ghost -- So be it and Beleis ---

## Nada

Blessed Sister of the Emerald Cross: Be ye blest of my presence - and of my being -- And be part of the plan which is now unfolding unto them -- For it shall be given unto us to sit in council and to be part of the "Great Plan" which has been prepared within the Inner Temple by the Most Worthy Grand Master -- And it shall be given unto us to have our part to fulfill that the great plan may be fulfilled -- And each and every one shall be portioned out as he is prepared to receive -- And so be it and Selah -- I am in the place wherein ye shall go and ye shall receive instructions in the eternal verities (Losoloes) and ye shall be unto thyself sufficient - and ye shall go and come at will -- And there shall be many within this place to receive thee and to sibor thee - for each has a part for thee which ye shall receive in the Name of the Most High Living God---

And ye shall be as one which has prepared thyself for thy part-- Is it not said that "Ye become that for which ye are prepared? And so be it and Selah -- I am come unto thee from out of the place wherein they sit in council -- And it is said that ye shall be brot out of the Earth in the time which is near and ye shall be given thy assignment which shall take thee back into the "world of men" -- And that ye shall be unto them that which we have been unto thee ---

And that them which are so prepared may receive within the place wherein they are - that which they are prepared to receive -- And so be it and Beleis -- Be ye as one which has received thy inheritance in full -- And be ye at peace and poise - and ye shall receive of the Father - Son and Holy Ghost -- So be it and Beleis -- Blest are they which are prepared to receive thee - for as they receive

114

thee shall they receive the Father and Mother Sarah -- And so be it and Beleis ---

Go ye into the world of men prepared to be unto them their hands and their mouth - for as ye receive of them shall ye give unto them which are prepared to receive -- So be it in the name of the Most High -- It is given unto me to be one which has groomed thee for thy new part and I am glad that ye have received thy inheritance and there shall be great rejoicing thruout the kingdom -- For as one is brot in it is cause for rejoicing -- And ye have had a foretaste of this joy - And such is it that when one is raised in the Inner Temple - that they come from many spheres and many planets that they may add their part --

And glorious is the music beyond words to describe and the light is splendor - and the organ which is not as anything known on Earth peals out its music which is heard in many spheres -- And it is given to some of Earth to hear it which are so attuned -- And so be it that some shall be so attuned that they may hear - for blest are they which do hear -- And it shall be given unto many to see the great manifestations which shall accompany the raising of the initiate within the Inner Temple -- And was it not given unto thee to witness an initiation of one so raised in the winter of 1956? And so shall ye come to know that which goes on about thee -- And so be it and Beleis -- And as ye have received of me so have ye received of the Father - Son and Holy Ghost -- So be it and Beleis --- I am thy Sister Nada of the Inner Temple and of the Order of the Emerald Cross --
-

Recorded by Sister Thedra --

# Part #44

Blest of may being: Be ye prepared to receive that which is prepared for thee by the one and only Brother Bor - and that which he has prepared for them -- And so shall ye receive it in the Name of the Father - Son and Holy Ghost -- So be it - Amen and Beleis ---

## Brother Bor

Blessed Sister of the Emerald Cross: And be ye blest of that which ye shall receive of me - and of the Father which has sent me unto thee -- And now it is come that the great barrier has been broken - and the great void is bridged - and that ye have been part of the great plan - it shall be given unto thee to pass freely - for ye shall be given that which shall serve as passport into all the secret places wherein ye shall go - and wherein ye shall receive the "Greater Part" - and for that have ye been prepared -- And so be it that ye shall be given a new part - and ye shall receive thy instructions within the place wherein I am - and ye shall return as my emissary - and ye shall receive that which ye shall give unto them which shall be prepared to receive thee in the Name of the Father - Son and Holy Ghost -- So be it that there shall be many which shall receive thee - and of thee -- As ye have received so shall ye give un unto them -- And they shall be blest which do receive -- And so be it and Beleis ---

And it shall be given unto them to be prepared to receive that which ye shall be given for them -- And so be it that they shall be lifted up and they shall be blest and they shall know that which they have received is of the Father - Son and Holy Ghost -- And so be it and Selah ---

116

I am come unto thee that ye may be brot into the place wherein I am - and that ye may receive that which is prepared for thee -- And so be it that ye shall be brot out of the Earth - and ye shall be as one of us - and ye shall be given as we are given - and ye shall know as we know -- And ye shall be equal unto us - for is it not given unto' thee thy. "Sonship" - and have ye not received thy inheritance -- And so shall ye be received as a Sister of the Inner Temple - and of the Emerald Cross - and as one of the Sisters of the Seven Rays -- For long have ye been prepared - and long have we awaited thy return -- So be it that we shall receive thee in love and joy -- And so be it and Beleis -- I am thy Brother Bor - and thy Sibor of the Inner Temple - and of the Emerald Cross and the Brotherhood of the 7 Rays ---

Blest of my being: Be ye prepared to receive that which has been prepared for them by our Brother Coro - and that which shall be given unto thee in the Name of the Father - Son and Holy Ghost -- Amen and Beleis ---

**Coro**

Blest of my being: Be ye blest of my presence - and be prepared to enter into my secret place - for I have kept a place for thee - and I shall be glad to receive thee -- And so be it and Beleis

Be ye as one which has passport into all the secret places of the Earth - and them which are not of the Earth -- And is it not a glorious new day when the great barrier has been broken - and the veil of maya has been removed - and wherein we shall sit in council together -- And ye shall come into my place as freely as into thy own stores wherein they sell the "toys of men" ---

117

And so they come to know how small are their toys -- And they shall be given to know what we mean when we say: "the children of Earth" for they are as little children which have not gone out from their place of birth -- They know not that which is beyond their little walls which have imprisoned them - And so shall they come to know that theirs is a large omniverse - wherein are many worlds which are inhabited with people which are free - and which know their Source - and which are not bound - and which have the fortune of the Father - and which can and do go and come freely -- They need no passport and they carry no portfolio – yet they are within the Earth and they are as the ones which have the power and the knowledge to deliver thee out of thy own self-created darkness ---

So be it that they shall bring unto them which are prepared to receive that which shall break their bond and deliver thee out of darkness -- Ye shall come to know how small is thy "Red Star" - and as ye have known no other or as ye have no memory of any other place - ye cannot comprehend the darkness and the smallness of thy world -- And ye shall be prepared to know - for as ye are prepared ye shall stand on the "High Holy Mount" - and ye shall see her pass out of her present port into her new berth ---

And ye shall be glad for her new part and for her freedom! For long has she cried as one bound - and in darkness - and now she shall be delivered - and she shall be prepared in peace and joy - for the new habitations which are being prepared to share her new glory -- And so be it that ye shall come to know that which goes on about thee -- And so be it and Selah ---

I am come unto thee which are prepared to receive me - that ye shall be unbound - and that ye may see with the greater vision - and that ye may know that which ye have seen -- And so be it that ye shall be glad for thy preparation -- And so be it and Selah -- I am thy Brother Coro - of the secret place wherein the records are - and wherein ye which are prepared may enter -- So be it and Selah ---

Blest of my being: Be ye prepared to receive that which shall be given unto them by our Sister of Light Saboni -- And it shall be given in the Name of the Father - Son and Holy Ghost -- Amen and Beleis ---

## Sister Saboni

Blest of my presence and of my being: And be ye as ones which can comprehend that which I say unto thee - for it is given unto me to be thy Sibor - and I am sent unto thee of the Father - that ye may receive of Him - And as He has sent me ye shall receive in His Name -- And in the time which is near I shall come into the Earth and I shall give unto thee that which ye are prepared to receive -- For it is said that many shall be sent and I have asked that I be one so chosen -- And as it is given unto me to know them wherein I shall go and to claim them as my own -- I shall be glad to go unto them that they may know wherein they are staid - and that they may receive the "Greater Part" - and for that am I prepared - for it is given unto me to know the depth of despair within the place wherein I shall go - and the darkness which has been unto them their sorrow---

And will it not be given unto us to deliver them? For it is said that they shall be prepared to receive -- And so be it and Beleis -- I am glad that I shall be given passport unto them - and I am glad that they shall be prepared - and therein shall be much joy! And so be it and Beleis ---

119

I am one which has guarded and loved the land wherein I shall go - and wherein I shall work with all my being - that she shall be delivered out of bondage - for she shall be one of the parts which shall dip under and she shall be rent in twain - and she shall not be as she is - for she shall be as the boot torn away -- And she shall not give footing to man for many an age - for she shall rest beneath the waters - and she shall not give comfort unto them which I call my own - and she shall be a part of the old order past -- And so be it and Beleis ---

And as I shall come unto the Earth for a part which shall be given unto me of the Father - I shall complete it and return into my place before the day of chaos -- And ye shall be prepared to receive me - and ye shall be prepared to be delivered up - for therein is wisdom - - And ye shall not know sorrow and suffering - them which are prepared to be delivered -- And so be it and Beleis -- Blest shall they be which are prepared to receive me - for I shall be unto them that which shall be unto them their deliverance -- And so be it and Beleis ---

I am thy Sister Saboni - Guardian of Italy - and of the Inner Temple and of the order of the Emerald Cross ---

Blest of my being: Be ye at peace and poise - and be ye prepared to receive that which is given unto thee by our blessed Mother Sarah - for She has prepared a part for them - which shall be given unto them in the Name of the Father - Son and Holy Ghost -- So be it and Beleis ---

120

## Blessed Mother Sarah

Blest of my being: Be ye at peace and poise - for I am come that the world of men may know "Peace and Poise" - and that they may be reminded of their heritage -- And so shall they know their place from which they have gone out -- Now it is given unto them to be in darkness - yet they shall be delivered out -- <u>And for that are many being sent out from the Inner Temple that they may know they "are not alone"</u> -- And so be it that they shall be gathered together and they shall receive that which shall be fortuned unto them of the Father - Son and Holy Ghost -- So be it and Selah -- I am come unto thee in peace and that ye may partake of my Peace and Poise - for it is given unto me to be thy Mother - and ye have not remembered me and ye have not remembered thy heritage - for it is given unto thee to be "poor in spirit" -- And ye have given no credit unto them which are thy Benefactors - and so be it that ye shall be reminded of them---

And now ye shall give unto them recognition and thanks - for they have kept thee and they have watched thy progress - and they have supplied thy needs -- And now they stand ready to deliver thee out of the straits of darkness wherein shall be much sorrow - <u>And so be ye wise and give unto them credit for thy well-being - and ye shall be blest -- Are ye not mindful of them which have supplied thee water and fresh air</u> -- And are ye not mindful of thë blessed Polaris which has kept the Earth on which ye stand in perfect balance? And the mighty Hasma - which has been unto the Earth that which is sufficient unto Her that She may give comfort unto Her habitation -- And so be ye reminded of them when ye are comforted and fed -- And when ye are discomforted shall ye not call unto them

- and so be it that they shall hear thee and they shall be unto thee that which shall profit thee - And so be it and Beleis ---

Be ye as one which remembers thy heritage and be glad for thy remembering - for it shall be given unto thee as ye will it -- And be ye of a mind to remember and to return unto the Source - and ye shall be blest of the Father and of thy Mother -- And so be it and Selah--

I am of mind to receive ye into the place from which ye have gone out - and be ye of a mind to return -- And there shall be great joy and much gladness -- And be ye one which is given unto peace - for  as ye send out so shall it return unto thee three fold -- And be ye given to say that which shall lift up thy brother -- For it is the law - "As ye give so shall ye receive" -- And so be it such as shall profit thee -- And be ye blest of the Father - Son and Holy Ghost -- I am thy Mother Sarah - and the fortune of the Father –

Recorded by Sister Thedra ---

# Part #45

Blest of my being: Be ye prepared to receive that which is prepared for thee by our blessed Brother of Light Maheru -- And that which he has for them shall be given unto them in the Name of the Father - Son and Holy Ghost -- So be it and Beleis ---

## Maheru*

Blessed Sister of the Emerald Cross - and of the School of the "Seven Rays"-- Was it not given unto me to receive thee into the "Order of the Seven Rays?" And have I not stood sponsor for thee? And so be it that I await to receive thee into the place wherein I am - and ye shall be as one returned from a long sojourn within the places of darkness -- For it is given unto me to remember thee before thy Earthly journey began -- And I know that which ye have forgotten -- And so be it ye shall remember -- And as ye have given of thyself that others may be lifted up - so do I give unto thee -- And so be it that ye shall receive me unto thyself - as I am prepared to receive thee into my place -- For I shall come unto thee and ye shall know me - for have I not come unto thee within the place wherein ye are? And have I not given unto thee the spelling of the name which I now use? And have I not given of myself that ye may be brot into the place wherein I am? And so be it and Beleis ---

Be ye prepared to receive them which shall come into thee - for they shall bring thee into the place wherein I am -- And there shall be great joy and much gladness -- So be it and Beleis -- I say unto them - that there shall be a great gathering in - a great coming together - and there shall be remembering - and there shall be great

123

rejoicing! For it is the day of rejoicing when all things shall be made new - a new Earth - a new heaven - a new body - and a new place of abode! And ye have not dreamed of the richness of thy heritage---

And the day is come when man and angel shall sit in council - and they shall sip together - and they shall remember that which they have said in their sleep -- So be it that there is cause for rejoicing and therein is wisdom -- <u>So be ye at peace and poise - for there are many which stand ready to be unto thee thy hands and thy feet -- Ye have but to reach out in love and thanksgiving</u> - So be it that ye shall be blest of them and as they have remembered thee in thy darkness so shall ye be mindful of them -- And so be it and Selah ---

And for the first time I say unto thee that it has been given unto me to go the "Royal Road" - and that I have come into the place wherein the Father is - in full consciousness of my being and of my inheritance without tasting death - For it was given unto me to make my ascension within the past few years - and ye shall be privileged to know that which I experienced -- And ye shall be as one so prepared -- For it is the plan which our blessed Brother of Light - Sananda - the Son of God the Father - has given into us so long ago - yet the age had not come when man should accept it -- And now in the New Day - the New Age - it shall be given unto many to go the Royal Road -- And so be it and Selah ---

I am come that ye may be prepared to partake of that which we of the Royal Assembly have to offer thee -- So be it given unto thee in the Name of the Most High Living God -- So be it and Selah -- I am thy Sibor and thy Brother of the Brotherhood of the Seven Rays - and the Order of the Emerald Cross - Maheru - (*formerly known as Muru)

Blest of my being: Be ye prepared to receive that which is prepared for them by our blessed Brother of Light - Marshea - for he has given it unto them in the Name of the Father - Son and Holy Ghost - So be it and Beleis ---

## Marshea

Blest of my being and of my presence: I am come unto thee that ye may give unto them which I have received of the Father for them - and as I receive of Him I shall give unto thee -- And they shall be prepared to receive that which shall be given unto them -- For in the time which is near I shall come into the Earth - into the world of men - and I shall pass among them - and I shall seek out them which I have watched - and which I have marked - and which are ready to receive me - and they shall know me -- For as I am prepared to come unto them - so shall they be prepared to receive me - for I shall come in the Name of the Father which shall send me - and they shall be quickened - and they shall be given to remembrance -- And for this shall I go out from my place of abode - and I shall be unto them the hands of the Father made manifest -- So be it and Beleis ---

Be ye prepared to receive me - for I shall come unto thee and ye shall know me - and I shall give unto thee that which I have for thee -- So be it and Selah -- I am one which has given of myself that ye may be prepared for the Inner Temple -- So be it that there are many which have groomed thee -- And so be it that ye shall be blest of them -- And so be it that ye shall be brot into the secret place of the Most High Living God - and ye shall receive of the Father - Son and Holy Ghost -- So be it and Beleis -- I am thy Brother and Sibor - Marshea - of the Order of the Emerald Cross ---

125

Blest of my being: Be ye prepared to receive that which I shall give unto thee - that they may receive or me and of the Father which has sent me unto them -- And so be it given in His Name -- So be it and Beleis ---

## Sananda

Blest of my presence: I say unto thee that I am in the world of men -- I am in a garment of flesh - of flesh and bone am I -- And I have come that my covenant shall be fulfilled - for have I not given unto thee my word that I should come? And that I should go to prepare a place - and I should return to claim my own? Now that I am come ye shall not deny me - for it is given unto me to be the "Director of This Show" -- And I am in the place wherein I am for that which shall be given to me to do of the Father - And it shall be given unto many to receive me - and unto me to receive them into my secret place of abode -- And we shall counsel together - and there shall be great revelations and great accomplishments -- And there shall be signs and manifestations of my presence - and as ye are prepared so shall I reveal myself unto thee -- And so be it and Beleis---

I am the porter at the gate - and I see that none pass which are unprepared -- And as I come unto thee out of my secret place of abode - I use the sign of the three pyramids - and as I am in another place I omit them ---

And now it is given unto me to be in another place wherein are many which sit in council that ye may come into thy rightful place - and that ye may be quickened - and that ye shall receive thy sonship -- And have I not said that "There are none within this place which are not my equal - for have they not too received their sonship?"

126

And as for them which shall cry: anti-Christ - where is thy fortune of learning? Wherein have ye been sibored in the way of the wise? Wherein have ye known the Christ? And as ye give unto thyself credit for so much - ye shall begin with thyself - and I ask thee: Who art thou? And whence cometh thou? And whither goest thou?

And ye shall stand mute - for ye know not -- And I am come that ye may know thyself - and as ye have not known the Father nor thyself - ye have not known me ---

And so be ye prepared to receive me -- And ye shall be as one searching in a dark closet to read the "Book of the dead" - for it is now the day of the New Age - when I walk as man in the flesh -- And I give unto thee that which is Living Water and Living Bread which is full of substance -- And ye have but to receive it in the Name of the Father - Son and Holy Ghost -- And it shall be unto thee all things!

And for them which cry: Jesus! Jesus Christ! They shall be as ones which seek in the dark recesses of the past - for was it not given unto me - the Man of Galilee - to know thee - and have I not gone the long way to bless thee? And have I not given of myself that ye may be in the world to usher in the new day - and that ye may fulfill thy mission and return unto thy Source?

And now it is given unto me to be of a New Order - of a new dispensation -- And have I not been sent that the new plan may be fulfilled? And as I have returned unto thee - I bear a new name which has been given unto me of my brothers in the Inner Temple __ And I say unto thee that I am he which was sent unto thee in the days of the past wherein they martyred their saviors - and wherein they crucified their benefactors! Now it is come that they shall not martyr them which are sent of the Father - but they shall receive them in honor and dignity -- So be it and Beleis -- I am thy Sibor and thy Benefactor - one which ye shall come to know as Sananda ---

Blest of my being: Be ye prepared to receive that which is prepared for thee by the one and only Beautealu - and it shall be given unto them in the Name of the Father - Son and Holy Ghost -- So be it and Beleis ---

**Beautealu**

Blessed one: <u>Be ye at peace and poise - and ye shall receive of the Father</u> - Son and Holy Ghost -- So be it and Beleis --

I am come that ye may receive that which I have kept for thee - - So be ye as one which has received thy inheritance - and so be it that it shall be cause for great rejoicing - and so be it and Selah -- Be ye as one which is prepared for the Inner Temple - and there shall be many to receive thee -- And so be it and Selah ---

And now it is come that there shall be a great learning - and a great speaking - and a great awakening - and a great gathering in - and there shall be much gladness! And so be it and Selah -- And as I am one which has given of myself that this shall be accomplished - I too - shall have my reward - for only they which have been privileged to see them gathered in - know the joy and gladness which is their only reward for waiting! So be it that ye shall partake of my joy and gladness - for ye shall stand upon the High Holy Mount and ye shall see as we thy Sibors see -- And ye shall know even as we know -- And so be it and Beleis ---

Be ye as one which has finished thy sojourn in the realms of darkness - and as one which has returned unto thy Source - and ye shall be brot out of darkness - and ye shall return into darkness no more -- So be it and Selah ---

And now it is come that ye have received thy inheritance in full - ye shall have free concourse into all the secret places of Earth - and ye shall be given thy shield which shall serve as passport unto them which are not of the Earth -- And ye shall be free to go and come at will - and ye shall be free from the gravitation of the Earth and free from the attraction of the moon -- And therein is freedom and mastery -- So be it and Beleis -- And this is part of thy inheritance given unto thee of the Father and of the Mother-- So be it and Selah - I am thy Sibor and Older Brother of the School of the Seven Rays - Beautealu ---

Blest of my being: Be ye prepared to receive that which shall be given for them by our blessed Brother Bor - for he has a part which has been prepared for them in the Name of the Father - Son and Holy Ghost -- Amen and Beleis ---

**Brother Bor**

Blest of my being and of my presence: Be ye at peace and poise - and ye shall receive of the Father - Son and Holy Ghost -- So be it and Selah ---

Be ye as one which has returned unto the Father and Mother - and ye shall receive of Them that which They have kept for thee -- And so be it and Selah -- I am come that ye may be brot out of darkness - and that ye may know that which is thy inheritance -- For

129

the Father has willed it that ye be given full communication and full concourse into His place of abode - and that ye shall remember thy being in the place wherein He is and the part which ye had with Him before going into darkness -- And have ye not remembered them - thy Father and Mother - in thy longing? And have ye not dreamed of thy day with Them? And for that have ye been better! And will it not be given unto thee to be received of Them - and will ye not be purified as ye were even before going out into darkness?

For it has been given unto thee to gather about thee the mass which ye call the body - or the pore - and which is of Earthly substance - and which shall be purified - and which shall become as light substance - and ye shall pass out of the denser part into the light substance -- And ye shall become as one made new - and as one resurrected or as one transformed -- And ye shall not know death - nor that which ye have called death -- For ye shall step forth into thy glorified body made new -- And as ye have received so shall ye give unto others - for it shall be given unto thee the power to command the elements of Earth and they shall obey in love and harmony -- So be it and Beleis ---

And it is come that there shall be many which shall call unto thee - and as they call ye shall respond - and as they are prepared so shall they receive - and such is part of thy new part -- And so be it and Selah -- And now it is given unto me to be one of thy Sibors - and as I have sponsored thee I am responsible for thee -- And as ye are responsible unto me and ye are now sent out unto them from the place wherein I abide - ye shall remember that which ye have learned and that which ye have been given in the Inner Temple -- And ye shall be true unto thy trust - and ye shall go into darkness no

130

more -- So be it that ye shall return into this place at will - and ye shall receive as ye ask -- And so be it and Beleis ---

I am as one which stands ready to serve thee in the name of the Most High Living God -- So be it and Beleis -- I am thy Brother Bor - of the Inner Temple -- So be it and Selah ---

Recorded by Sister Thedra of the Emerald Cross –

# Part #46

Blest of my being: Be ye prepared to receive that which is for them by the One and only Coro -- He has prepared it for them in the Name of the Father - Son and Holy Ghost -- So be it and Beleis---

## Brother Coro

Blest of my presence: I am come that the Father's will may be done thru me - that ye may receive of Him - and of the Son and Holy Ghost -- So be it and Selah ---

And as ye have given of thyself that others may receive of Him - great shall be thy reward - for have ye not received that which He has willed thee? And have ye not returned unto Him -- So be it and Beleis -- And for that am I glad - for we have waited long to receive thee - and so be it our waiting is ended -- So be it ye shall be received into the place of the Most High Living God -- And ye shall walk within the Light of the Christ - made whole -- So be it and Beleis ---

And now ye shall go and come at will into all the places of the Earth - and ye shall be given that which shall serve as passport into all the Temples thruout the Father's Kingdom - and so be it there are many ---

And be ye as one which knows wherein ye are staid -- And so be it that ye shall know as we know - and ye shall remember as we remember -- And ye shall receive as we receive of the Father - Son and Holy Ghost - So be it and Beleis -- And is it not said that ye shall give unto them as ye have received? And so be it -- And for that are ye prepared - for there has been many which has given of themself that ye may be prepared -- And so be it and Beleis ---

And ye shall go out into the world of men prepared to be unto them the hands and feet of the Father made manifest -- Ye shall touch them and they shall be made whole -- Ye shall speak that which the Father shall give unto thee and they shall be made new -- And ye shall be unto thyself true -- Ye shall give unto them as the Father shall give unto thee -- And ye shall be as the one sent out from the Inner Temple which has been given thy inheritance - that the Father's will may be done in thee and thru thee and by thee - and for thee -- So be it and Selah ---

I am one which has awaited thy coming - and now that ye have received thy inheritance - ye shall be brot into the place wherein I am - and ye shall receive of me that which I have kept for thee - and there shall be much joy and gladness -- So be it and Beleis -- And for this have we waited -- And be ye as one made new - and ye shall receive as we thy Sibors receive of the Father - Son and Holy Ghost -- And ye shall see the Light of the Christ - and ye shall walk therein and ye shall return into darkness no more -- So be it and Beleis ---

I am one of thy Sibors which has been given unto waiting - and I am glad to receive thee into the inner place of my abode -- And so be it and Beleis ---

I am thy Brother Coro - of the Order of the Emerald Cross --

Blest of my being: Ye shall now be blest of the one and only Posied - and that which he has for thee -- And ye shall give it unto them for therein is wisdom -- And so be it and Beleis ---

133

**The Posied**

Blessed Sister of the Emerald Cross: Have I not watched thy progress- and waited this day? For it is given unto me to be one of thy Sibors -- Have I not sibored thee in the temples of the Lotus? And have I not seen thee upon the altars in the land of the East? And have I not waited for this day? And so shall it be a time of rejoicing - and great shall be the rejoicing!

For as one is raised into the Inner Temple there is joy untold! And many come from many planets to receive them -- And so be it and Selah -- I am one which has guarded thee and which has given of myself that this may be accomplished ---

And now that ye have received thy inheritance - ye shall come into my place of abode and ye shall be as a guest in my house -- And ye shall know as we know -- And there shall be no more secrets - no more darkness - no more sorrow - and no more longing -- For ye shall see the Light of the Christ and ye shall walk therein -- And so be it and Selah ---

Be ye as one which has received that which has been willed unto thee of the Father - and ye shall go and come at will into His place of abode -- And ye shall be given passport into all the temples within the Father's realm - and ye shall stand free forevermore! And ye shall not be bound by the laws of the Earth and ye shall be free from the attraction of the moon -- And ye shall go into darkness no more -- And ye shall receive as we receive of the Father and the Son and the Holy Ghost -- So be it and Selah ---

I am thy Sibor and thy Older Brother - the Posied - of the Emerald Cross ---

Blest of my being: Now ye shall receive that which our beloved Zamu has for thee - and it shall be added unto the others - for it shall be given unto them which await that which shall be unto them succor -- And so be it given unto them in the Name of the Father - Son and Holy Ghost -- Amen and Beleis ---

**Blessed Zamu**

Blest of my being: Be blest of my presence - and of the Father - Son and Holy Ghost -- For I am come that my light may be added unto thine that ye may receive the Father - Son and Holy Ghost --

And for this have we thy Sibors waited -- And so be it our waiting is ended -- And now ye shall be received into the Holy of Holies -- And there shall be no more longing - no more sorrow - no more suffering - for ye shall stand free - as we which have gone the Royal Road -- And ye shall be given as we are given -- Ye shall know as we know -- And as we receive of the Father - Son and Holy Ghost - so shall ye too receive -- And ye shall see the Light of the Christ and walk therein forevermore -- And ye shall go and come at will - and ye shall go into all the places of the Earth - and ye shall be free to enter into all the secret places of the Earth - and ye shall be free to enter into all the secret temples within the Father's place of abode -- And ye shall be given that which shall serve thee well -- For ye shall have no bondage and no limitations -- For this have ye been prepared - and for this have we thy Sibors worked - and our joy shall know no bounds -- So be it that ye shall be brot into my place of abode - and ye shall not want nor shall ye weary - for I am

135

prepared to be host unto thee -- And I have been host to many of the Royal Assembly -- So be it that I am prepared to receive thee in love and joy - and in the Name of the Most High Living God -- So be it and Beleis ---

I am thy Brother Zamu of the Emerald Cross ---

Blest of my being: Ye shall send these greetings out together - and ye shall add our blessed Brother Carneu's unto them -- So be it given unto them in the Name of the Father - Son and Holy Ghost -- Amen and Beleis ---

## Carneu

Blest of my being: Be ye blest of my presence and of my being -- I am come unto thee that ye may be prepared to receive of the Father - Son and Holy Ghost -- So be it and Beleis -- And as I come unto thee ye shall receive me in the Name of the Father - for it is given unto me to come unto thee from out of the silence that ye may know me - for I too have sibored thee - and I have not revealed unto thee my identity -- I shall now give unto thee my part which shall serve to bring thee close into the place wherein ye shall go -- And ye shall be as one welcomed home - for it is my great joy to see thee liberated ---

And ye shall come to know me as thy Brother Carneu - which is the name which has been given unto me - for I am within an eastern temple - or one of the secret places wherein ye shall go - and ye shall find me waiting to receive thee - and so shall there be gladness -- And so be it and Beleis ---

I am one which has given unto thee comfort - and of my love and of my service in the Name of the Father - and ye have not remembered -- And ye shall be glad for my deliverance for ye shall remember me as ye last saw me - and ye shall be glad that I too have received of the Father - Son and Holy Ghost -- So be it that I add my love and light into that of my blessed Brothers and Sisters -- So be it given unto thee as ye have prepared thyself -- And so be it I am glad and be it so - So be it and Beleis -- I am Carneu –

Blest of my being: Ye shall now receive that which our blessed Brother of Light has prepared for thee - and it shall be added unto the rest -- So be it given unto them in the Name of the Father - Son and Holy Ghost -- Amen and Beleis ---

**Marshan**

Beloved Sister of Light: Be ye blest of me and of my presence -- For I too have come out of the silence that ye may know me - and that ye may be welcomed into the place wherein I am -- And ye shall come to know me as thy Brother which has sibored thee in silence and love - and I asks nothing more than thy liberation and thy freedom from bondage -- So be it that the time is come - and ye shall stand free - And ye shall be brot into the place wherein I am - and ye shall remember me -- For it is given unto me to be one of thy Sibors within the past - and which has been blanked from thy memory---

Yet the time is come for remembering - and I am glad for thy return unto the Father -- For ye shall be free even as we are free -- And ye shall stand on the High Holy Mount and see as we see - and ye shall be glad for thy waiting - for have ye not been given that which shall serve thee well? So be it and Beleis ---

And now ye shall have free concourse into the place wherein I am - and ye shall go and come at will -- And so be it and Beleis -- Ye shall receive as we receive of the Father - Son and Holy Ghost -- Ye shall know as we know - and so be it that ye shall know no more darkness - no more sorrow - no more suffering - no more longing -- For ye shall see the Light of the Christ and walk therein forevermore -- So be it and Beleis ---

I am thy Brother and Sibor - Marshan - of the Emerald Cross - and the Brotherhood of the Seven Rays ---

Recorded by Sister Thedra ---

# Part #47

Blest of my being: Be ye at peace and poise and ye shall receive of me that which I am prepared to give unto thee -- And so be it given unto thee of the Father - Son and Holy Ghost -- So be it and Beleis -- Be ye as one which has presented thyself for preparation into the Inner Temple - and which has been groomed by thy Sibors -- And now it is given unto thee that which shall serve thee well - for it shall be unto thee thy shield and thy buckler - and thy passport into all the temples of the Father's realm - and into the places which are hidden from the unprepared ---

And so be ye as one which has received that which has been willed unto thee of the Father and Mother -- So shall ye enter into Their place of abode at will -- And ye shall be true unto thy office and ye shall give unto thy brothers as ye have received of us thy Sibors -- And ye shall have no false gods - nor shall ye ask of any man aught - for ye shall be sufficient unto thyself - and ye shall receive of the Father - Son and Holy Ghost - So be it and Beleis -- And ye shall see the Light of the Christ - and walk therein forevermore -- And ye shall know as we know - and ye shall receive as we receive -- So be it that ye shall know no more suffering - no more sorrow - no more darkness - no more longing -- For all thy longing shall be filled! And ye shall have thy new body without tasting of death -- And ye shall be free from the laws of the Earth - and the attraction of the Moon -- So shall ye be master of the elements of the Earth - and ye shall command them and they shall obey in love and harmony -- So be it and Beleis ---

I have given unto thee as the Father - Son and Holy Ghost - and as I have received -- And as ye have received of me - so shall they receive of thee as they are prepared -- So be it and Selah -- I am thy Brother and Sibor - Sananda ---

**Brother Esore**

Blessed one of the Emerald Cross - and of the Brotherhood of the Seven Rays: Have I not come unto thee from out of the silence that ye may know me? For from me have ye received that which shall serve thee well -- Ye shall come to know which is given unto thee by each of thy Sibors ---

For as ye have passed before them each has endowed thee with a special gift -- And I have withheld mine for this occasion -- Thy longing has been great - but it has been the better part of wisdom to withhold it -- And now ye shall receive it - and ye shall be glad for thy waiting -- For it is now come that ye shall receive thy inheritance in full -- And ye shall be given that which has been held in trust for thee -- And ye shall receive of the Father - Son and Holy Ghost -- And ye shall pass into the Temple wherein I am and ye shall know that which we know -- And ye shall be given free passport into the place wherein we are - and we shall be glad to receive thee. So be it and Beleis ---

I am thy Sibor and Brother and Benefactor - of the Order of the Emerald Cross -- Brother Esore ---

Blest of my being: Be ye prepared to receive that which is prepared for thee by our blessed Brother of Light - Maroni - for he has prepared a part which shall be given unto them in the Name of the Father - Son and Holy Ghost -- Amen and Beleis ---

**Maroni**

Blest of my presence - and of my being: I am come that they may be prepared to receive me - for I am prepared for this day -- And I too shall go out into the world of men - even as the brothers and sisters from the Inner Temple -- And I shall give unto them as I shall be given of the Father - for it is come that many shall be sent -- And they which are prepared shall receive the "Greater Part" And for that do we leave our present place of abode - and ye which are prepared shall receive of us which are sent -- And be ye as ones which are so chosen that ye may be the seed for the new Earth and the new heaven - for as ye are prepared so shall ye receive -- And be ye as ones which shall be prepared to receive us - for it is come when ye shall walk and talk with us which have worked ceaselessly for this day - and for the day when ye shall be prepared to receive us -- And for them so prepared they shall be brot into the secret place - and they shall be groomed for the "Greater Part" - and for that have I revealed myself ---

For in the days past there were few which were prepared to receive me - and that which was prepared for them - and it was given unto them to receive as they were prepared -- And now we shall begin again! And ye shall be given as ye are prepared to receive - for it is now the day of revelation ---

And the Earth shall give forth her secrets - and the vortex shall be broken - and ye shall read the records which are contained therein -- And so be it that the Father has willed it that ye shall know the

141

wonders of the Earth - and be master thereof -- And it shall be given unto many to prepare thee - and as it is given unto me to be one of them - I shall endeavor to bring thee out of thy place into my place of abode wherein ye may receive of thy inheritance in full - and therein is wisdom -. And so be it and Beleis ---

Before thee is a plan - and it is unfolding before thee - And now it is given unto thee to be in darkness - yet ye shall be brot out - and ye shall be quickened and ye shall know that which is thy inheritance -- Ye shall be blest of the Father and Mother - ye shall receive of the Father - Son and Holy Ghost - and ye shall become one with the Father - and such is thy inheritance -- And ye shall receive thy sonship -- So be it and Belsis ---

I am thy Brother and thy Sibor - Maroni - of the Emerald Cross and of the School of the Seven Rays -- And so be it and Selah ---

**Brother Teberus**

Beloved: Ye shall receive of the part which I have for thee - for it is given unto me to be one of thy Sibors and guardians -- I have come that ye may know me - and that ye may receive my greeting -- And so be it that my place of abode shall be open unto thee - and it shall contain no secrets -- For ye shall know as we know - ye shall receive as we receive - and ye shall partake of the manna which is our heritage -- And ye shall be one of us ---

So be ye prepared to receive of our love and of our joy - for ye shall be given of the Father - Son and Holy Ghost -- And there shall be much rejoicing - and great gladness and we shall be glad thy day of deliverance is come -- And so be it and Beleis ---

142

Now ye shall go into all the places of the Earth - and ye shall be received in the Father's Name - and in honor and dignity -- And ye shall have free communion with the Father - and with the Mother - and ye shall go and come at will -- And so be it and Beleis ---

I am thy Sibor and Brother of the Emerald Cross - Teberus ---

Blest of my being: Ye shall now receive of our beloved Brother which has prepared a part for them - and it shall be given unto them in the Name of the Father - Son and Holy Ghost -- So be it and Beleis ---

**Brother Joseph**

Blessed Sister of the Emerald Cross - and of the Brotherhood of the Seven Rays: Be ye blest of my being and of my presence -- For I am come that the Father's will may be done in me - thru me - by me - and for me -- And it is given unto me of Him that I may come unto thee - that they may be prepared to receive Him - thru me -- For it is said that many shall be sent into the Earth from the Inner Temple - and I am one of them -- And so shall I reveal myself unto them which are prepared to receive me -- And so be it and Beleis ---

I am one which has worked in silence for this day - and now it is come that many shall sit in council with me - and they shall know me as I know them - for I have not had my memory blanked from me - and I have remembered them from the beginning of their earthly journey ---

And it shall be a glad time of gathering together -- And there shall be great revelation for them prepared to receive -- And so be it

143

and Beleis -- Before ye were called out from among them it was given unto me to come unto thee - and I gave unto thee a token which was not of the Earth - and I said unto thee: "This is not of the Earth - and ye shall carry it as a talisman - and ye shall show it to no man" -- And ye have been true unto thy trust -- And as ye have been faithful in little things - so shall ye be given greater ---

And so be it that ye shall be prepared to receive that which I have kept for thee - for as ye have given me credit for being what I am I shall receive thee into the place wherein I am - and ye shall be given as we are given of the Father and ye shall receive of our love - and our joy -- For we shall rejoice in thy freedom and in thy fortune which shall be given unto thee -- And ye shall see the Light of the Christ and walk therein -- So be it and Beleis -- I am thy Brother and thy Benefactor - Joseph - of the School of the Seven Rays - and of the Emerald Cross –

Blest of my being: Be ye prepared to receive that which I have prepared for them - for it is the better part of wisdom that they receive that which I have for them -- And so be it given in the Name of the Father - Son and Holy Ghost -- So be it and Beleis ---

Blessed ones which are my sheep - which are given unto me of the Father and Mother: Be ye blest of my presence and of my being - for I am come that ye may receive me - and as ye receive me so shall ye receive the Father -- And now it is come that ye shall know us which are sent out of the Father - and ye shall be brot out of darkness and ye shall receive of the Father - even as we which have received our sonship - and ye shall be gathered up - even as we are gathered ---

144

For it shall be given unto thee to have dominion over the Earth - and the elements thereof -- And ye shall become like unto the Father - and ye shall be as He is - and equal unto Him - and ye shall know freedom from bondage - and ye shall be as one which has received thy inheritance - for ye shall not want nor suffer more -- So be it part of thy inheritance - and ye shall be given that which is willed unto thee of the Father - for He has given unto thee that which should be unto thee all things - and ye have but to accept it in His name ---

And so be ye prepared to receive that which is offered unto thee in His name -- And many shall be sent unto thee from the Inner Temple - and I shall be one of them -- For I shall walk among thee - and I shall seek thee out - and I shall put a mark upon thy forehead and ye shall be known unto them which shall follow me -- And so be it and Beleis ---

I have given unto thee my word - and it shall not return unto me void -- And so be it and Beleis -- I am the Director - and the Sibor of the Sibors - and thy Brother - and thy servant - Sananda - of the Emerald Cross - and the Brotherhood of the Seven Rays --- Recorded by Sister Thedra ---

# Part #48

Blest of my being: Be ye prepared to receive that which is prepared for thee by our blessed Brother of Light - Bernard - and what he has prepared for them -- For it is given unto him to be one which is within one of the secret places in thy native land (U.S.A.) and he shall be one which shall receive thee into his place of abode -- And so shall ye come to know him and that which he is doing - and the part ye shall have with him -- For it is given unto him to be one which is prepared for this day -- And he has given of himself and of his love and of his wisdom that this secret place might be established - and maintained for the work which is now to be done -- So be it that ye shall be brot into his place of abode and ye shall receive of his love and wisdom - and of his hospitality -- So be it and Beleis --
-

## Bernard

Blessed Sister of the Emerald Cross: I am one which has been unto thee before ye were called out from among them - and ye have remembered me - and that which I have said unto thee ---

And I shall welcome thee into my secret place of abode - and ye shall be as one of us -- So shall ye receive of our love and wisdom which is part of our inheritance -- So be it and Beleis ---

And it shall be given unto thee to know that which has not been revealed before - for it was the better part of wisdom to withhold my identity - and yet ye knew that I was one of thy brothers - and for that have I watched thy progress -- And I have been prepared to give thee assistance as ye might need it -- And I am glad that ye have

146

been received into the Inner Temple and that ye have accepted that which has been offered in love - mercy and wisdom ---

And so be it that ye shall know us thy brothers which are within this temple of light -- And we are prepared to go out into the world of men when the hour strikes - and as we are called -- For it is given unto us to be alert - and at the service of our blessed Lord and Master - and as He has said: "We sleep not - for we are vigilant and true to our office" - and we give of our time and effort that His work may be accomplished -- And ye shall come to know that ye are not alone - and that ye have many hands and feet at thy service ---

So be it that ye shall be brot into this place in the time which is near -- So be it and Beleis -- I am thy Brother of the School of the Seven Rays - and of the Emerald Cross - Bernard ---

## Footnote

Blest of my being: Shall they too not know that which has been held in trust for them? And shall they too not know that we are not talking in riddles? And shall they not come to know that we of the secret places are not among their dead? And shall they not learn that we walk as flesh and bone - and that we are sent that they may not destroy themself? So be it that ye shall add my part unto that of our Brother Bernard's - and that they may know that we are not playing foolish games - for we are prepared to prove that which we have said -- And so be it and Beleis -- Sananda ---

Blest of my being: Be ye prepared to receive that which is prepared for them by our one and only Brother Bor - for he has prepared a part for them - and it shall be given unto them in the name of the Father - Son and Holy Ghost -- Amen and Beleis ---

**Brother Bor**

Beloved Sister of the Emerald Cross: Be ye blest of me - and of my presence - and be ye as my hands unto them -- For it is given unto me to say unto thee that which is given unto me of the Father -- And ye shall be as one which shall receive as we thy Sibors -- For it is come that ye shall be brot into the place wherein I am - and ye shall know as we know - and ye shall be as one of us -- And ye shall receive that which we have kept for thee - and ye shall be as one prepared to return unto them as my ambassador -- And ye shall be given that which shall serve thee as passport into all the places wherein ye shall go - and there shall be no man to stop thee -- And ye shall ask of no man his opinion - and ye shall be unto thyself sufficient - for it shall be given unto thee to receive of the Father - Son and Holy Ghost -- So be it and Selah ---

And now I say unto them: Be ye prepared to receive my ambassadors - for they shall be given the power and the authority to deliver thee out of bondage - and to deliver thee up -- And so be it that it shall profit thee to receive them in the name of the Father - Son and Holy Ghost -- So be it that they shall seek out them which are prepared to receive that which they shall bring unto thee - and they shall touch thee and ye shall be as one come alive -- And so be it and Beleis ---

Be ye of a mind to receive them - and they shall find thee -- And for them so prepared they shall be brot into the place wherein I am - and they shall be prepared for the Inner Temple - and to receive

148

the "Greater Part"-- So be it and Beleis -- And ye shall be given as ye are prepared to receive -- And so be it and Salah ---

I am thy Brother Bor - of the Inner Temple and of the Emerald Cross ---

Blest of my being: Ye shall now receive that which is prepared for them by our blessed Sister or Light - Nada - and that which she has prepared for them - which shall be given unto them in the name of the Father - Son and Holy Ghost -- So be it and Beleis ---

## Sister Nada

Beloved Sister of the Emerald Cross: Be ye blest of my being and of my presence -- And ye shall be given of the Father as it is given unto me -- And as ye shall receive of Him so shall ye give unto them which are prepared to receive -- For it is come that we shall walk together - and we shall talk together - and we shall be as coworkers of the Father - for it has been given unto me to be of the Inner Temple - and I shall help prepare thee - and ye shall enter into the place wherein the Father and Mother is - at will ---

And ye shall be given free passport into all the secret temples within the Earth - and ye shall be free to go and come between the planets within the galaxy -- And therein ye shall have freedom and mastery -- And so be it that the Father's Will may be done in thee - and by thee - and for thee -- And so be it and Beleis -- Be ye as one of us - and be ye as one which has received thy inheritance in full - - And so be it and Selah ---

149

Now I say unto them which as yet have not awakened: Be ye of a mind to awaken - and we shall give unto them that which shall serve to awaken thee - and as ye are able to receive so shall we give unto thee -- And so be it and Beleis -- I am one which has come into the world of men - and not so long ago have I received my freedom -- And I am privileged to go and come - and it shall be given unto me to assist in thy "willed estate" - and which shall be unto thee thy deliverance and freedom -- And for that am I prepared -- And so be it and Beleis ---

I say unto them: Be ye prepared to receive that which is offered unto thee - for it shall be unto thee thy deliverance and thy freedom -- For not in the history of man has such a change come about in so short a time - and ye have but to stand still and lock - and listen -- And so be ye prepared to receive of the new dispensation - and of them which are sent to bring it into fulfillment - and ye shall be greatly rewarded -- So be it and Beleis -

I am thy Sibor – and Sister of the Emerald Cross - Nada ---

Blest of my being: Be ye prepared to receive that which is prepared for them by our blessed Brother of Light - The Aryan - for he has kept this part for this time -- And so be it given in the name of the Father - Son and Holy Ghost -- So be it and Beleis ---

**The Aryan**

Be ye blest of me and of my presence - my blessed Sister of the Emerald Cross: For it is given unto me to be one which has watched thee lo the eons in which ye have wandered in darkness -- I have stood upon the hill of Golgotha with thee - we have shed bitter tears

150

together for the same cause -- We have gone into the homes of the sick and dying together - that they might be lifted up - and that they might know the Father -- We have given our physical bodies in martyrdom for the same Cause -- And it was given unto us to sit in the secret place wherein our blessed Lord and Master síbored us - and we were privileged to hear from His own lips His account of His initiation into the Inner Temple wherein our blessed Brother Bor is - and he is one of the Kumaras -- And so be ye prepared to receive of them all -- And so be it and Beleis -- --

And now again we come to the time of gathering together - and them which were in the "Upper Room" for the last supper - shall again sit with Him around the council table - and they shall again hear from Him His account of the time He has been separated from us -- It has been given unto me to be the "Wanderer" - the one which He commanded to tarry until His return -- Now it is given unto me to sit with Him as on the night before he was taken into bondage of the Romans -- And He has been unto me all things in my wandering - and in my waiting -- And now my longing is satisfied - and my waiting is ended - and I am glad ---

So be it that thy waiting has ended - and ye shall be brot into the place wherein we are - and ye shall be as one of us - for it is long since we have been together - and ye shall remember me - as I have remembered thee -- For I have had continuous memory - and I have seen them come into embodiment after embodiment and not remember their being - from whence they came -- And they are as ones wandering in their sleep - for they ask not whence they come nor whither they goest - they are content to wander as one dead on their feet---

And forget not they are the living dead - and are they not to be pitied? - for it is the hardest part of our work to reach the living dead - for they hear not - neither do the see! They are as ones neither dead nor alive! - and they have been called the "angels of hell" and rightfully so - for they are neither good nor bad - neither hot nor cold! And as the Master has said: "I would that ye were one or the other - for I cannot reach thee in the middle - for ye are neither hot nor cold"-- And so be it that they shall be given a part which shall awaken them -- They shall either awaken or go into deep sleep -- and so be it that they may awaken -- And for that have many revealed themself - many have come out of the silence that they may be awakened ---

And for that do we labor without ceasing -- So be it that they shall come to know us - and the veil shall be lifted - and we which have worked in silence shall be revealed unto them -- And so be it that it shall be in love and wisdom -- And so be it and Beleis ---

I am one of thy Brothers of the School of the Seven Rays - and of the Emerald Cross -- I am The Aryan --- Recorded by Sister Thedra ---

www.ingramcontent.com/pod-product-compliance
Lightning Source LLC
Chambersburg PA
CBHW060459280326
41933CB00014B/2794